let it go let it go

Benedikte Bjerre
let it go let it go

kunstverein
göttingen

MOUSSE PUBLISHING

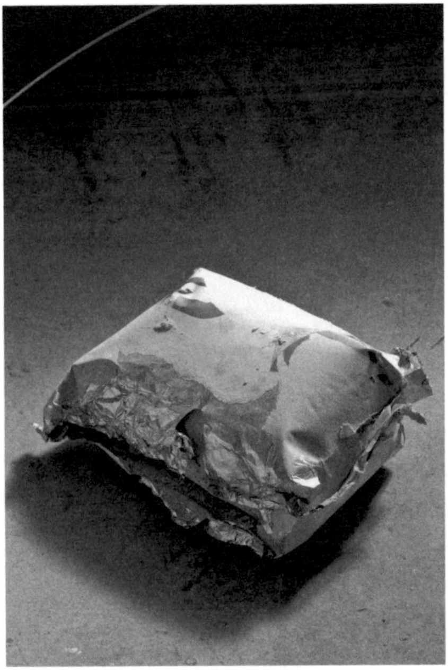

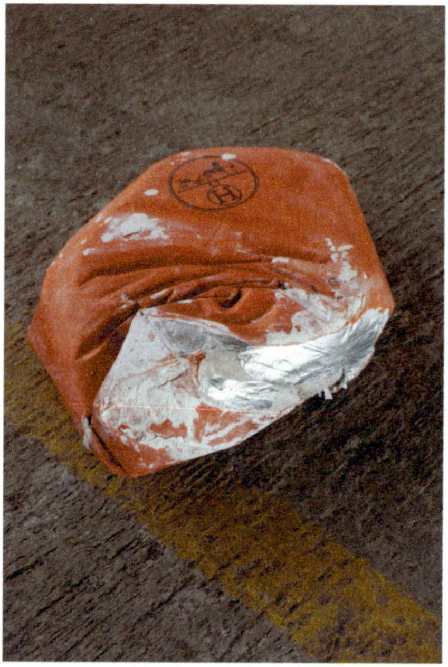

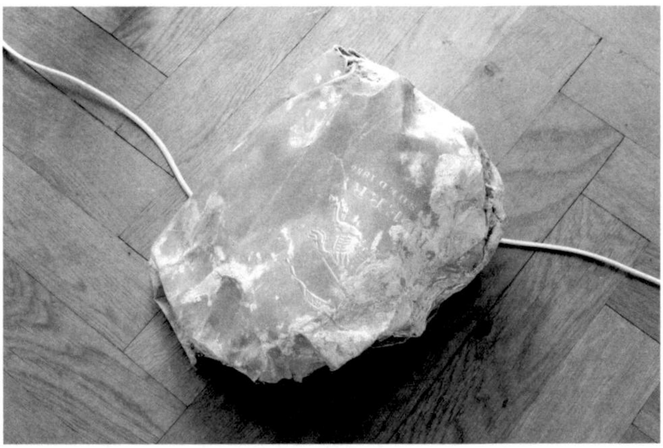

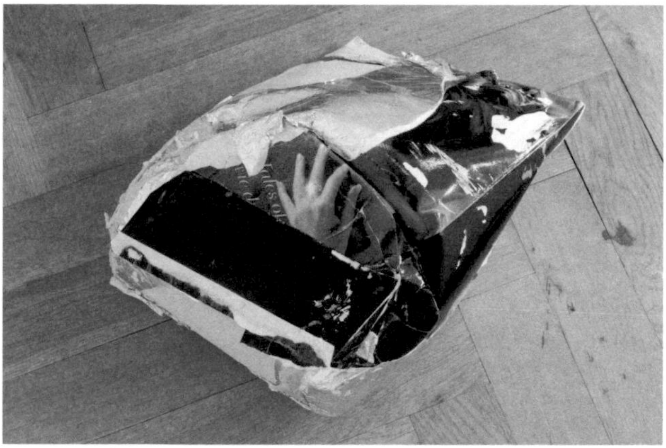

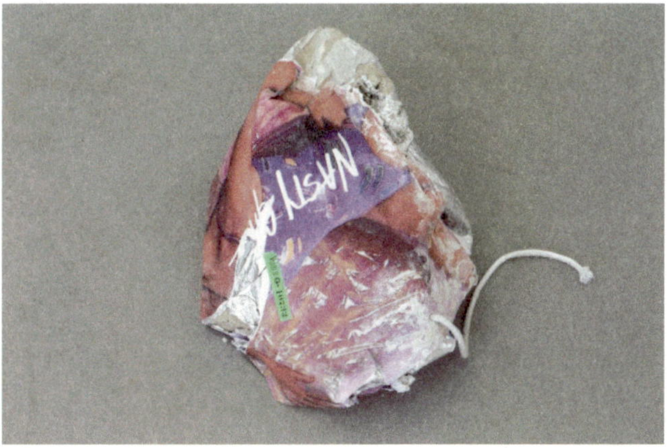

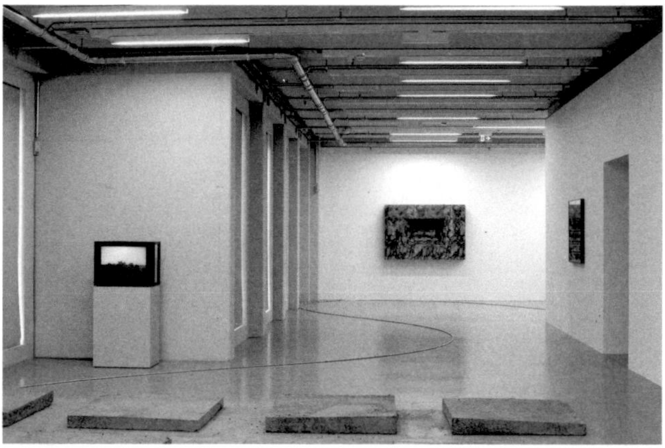

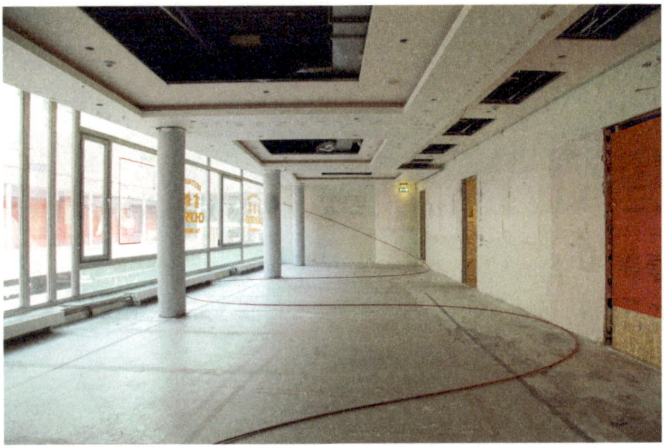

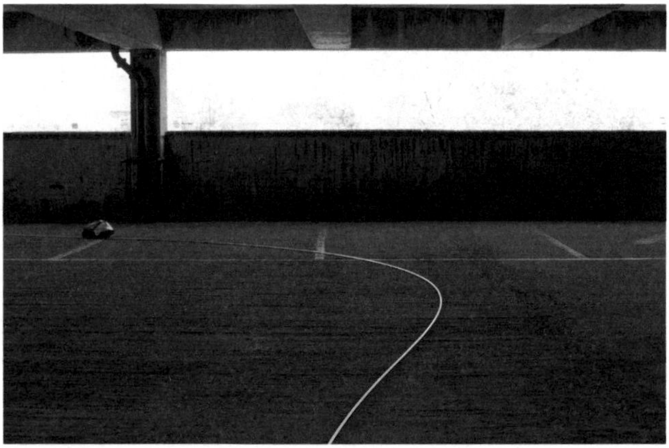

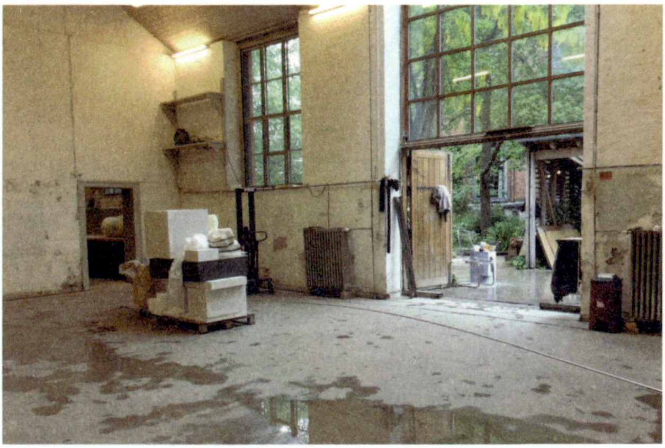

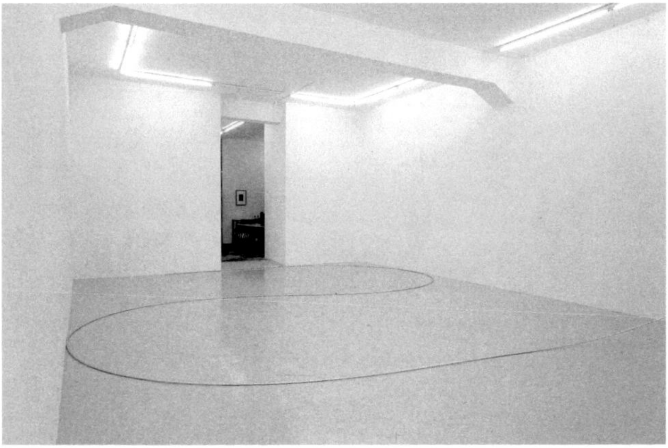

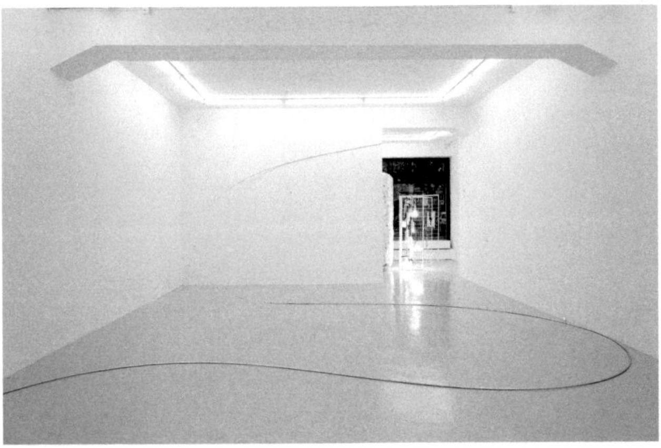

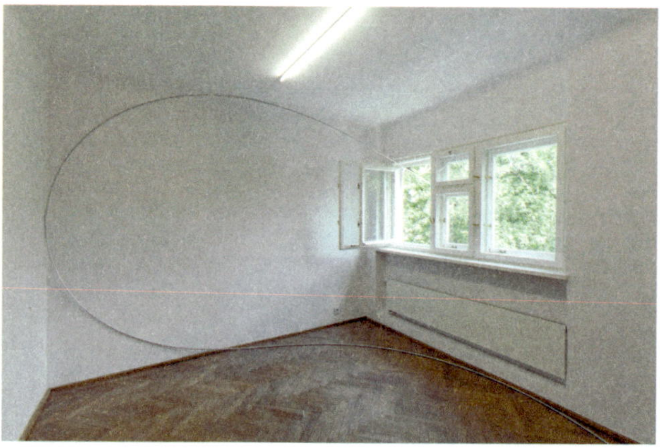

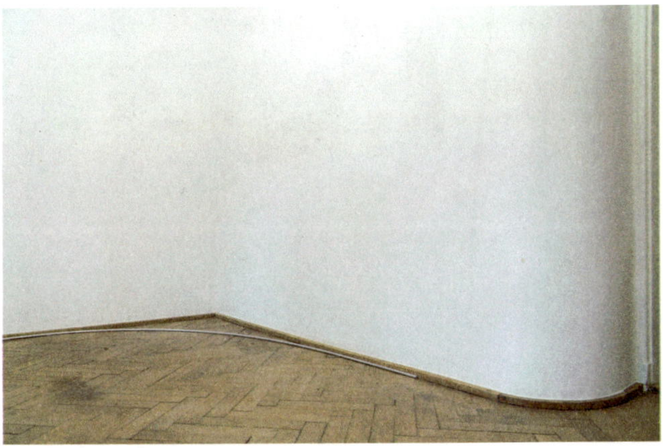

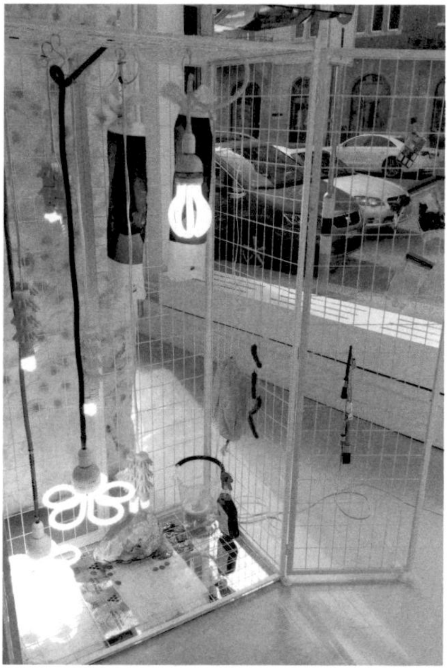

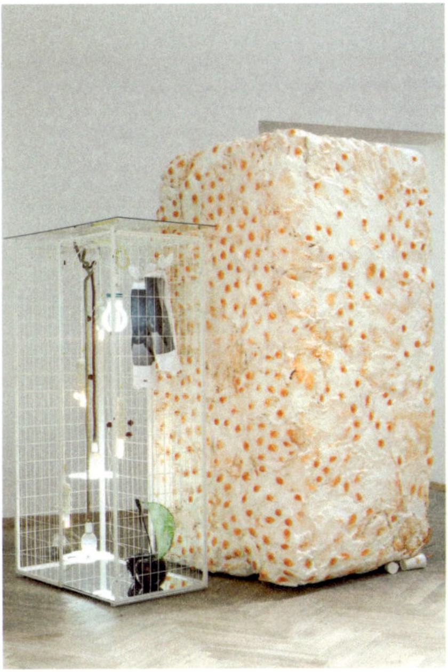

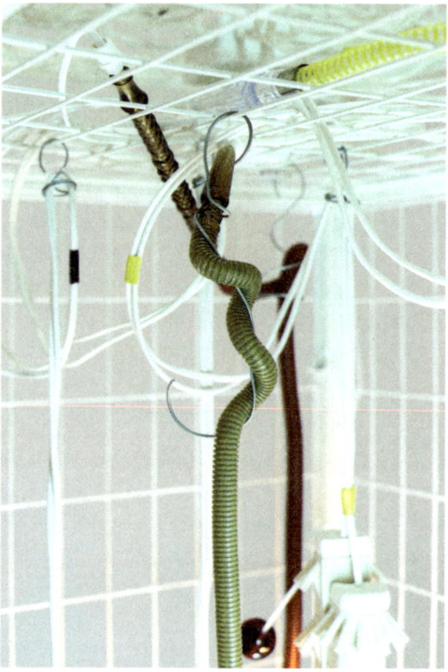

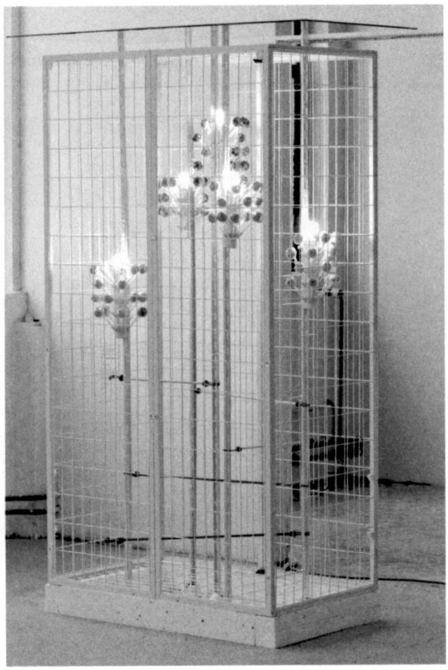

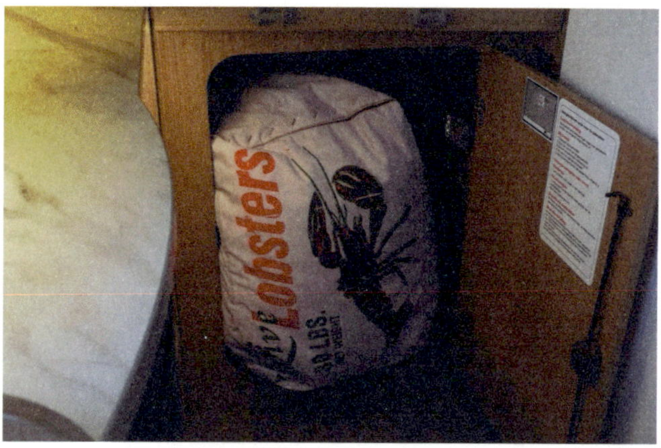
Lobsters

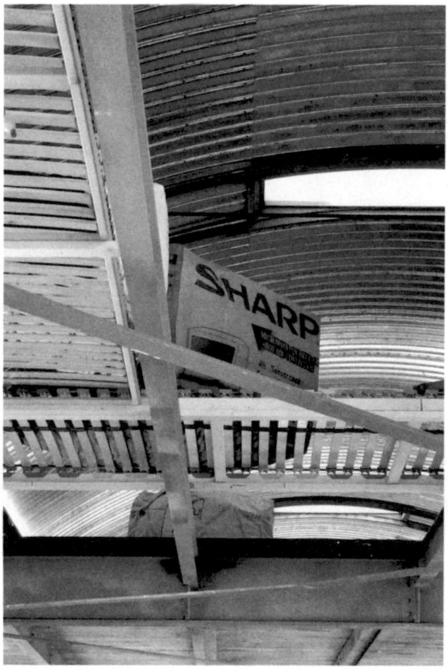
SHARP

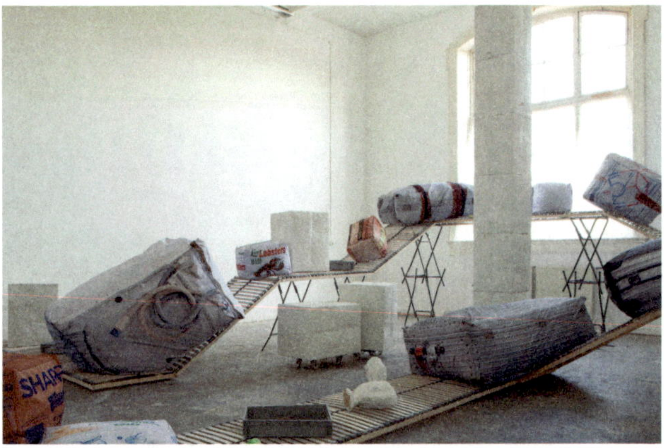

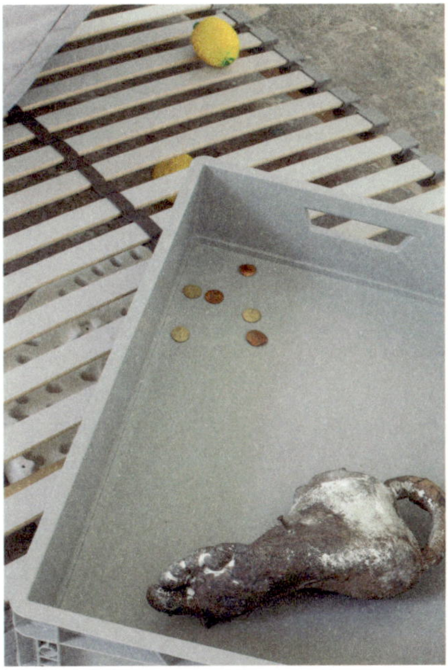

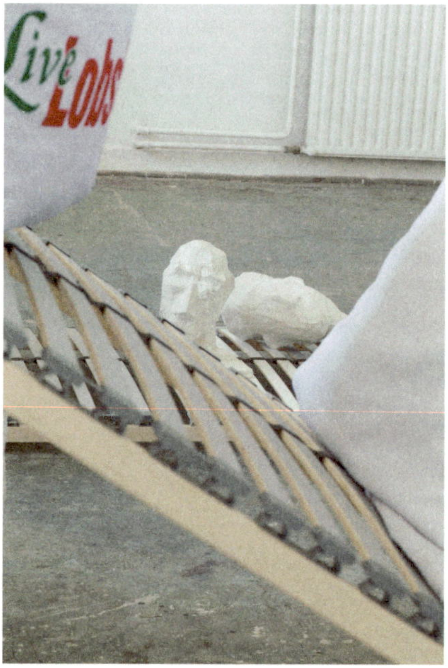

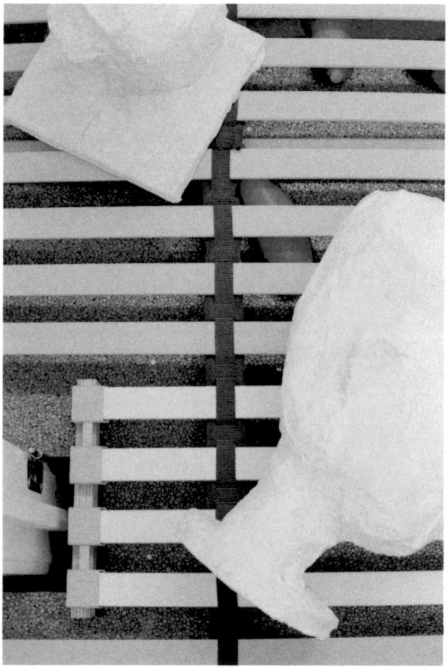

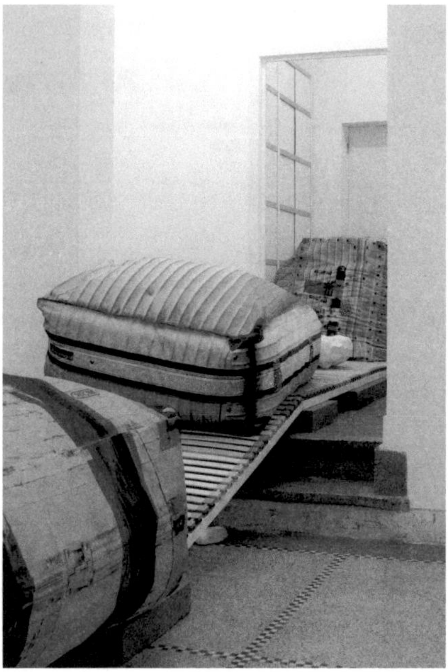

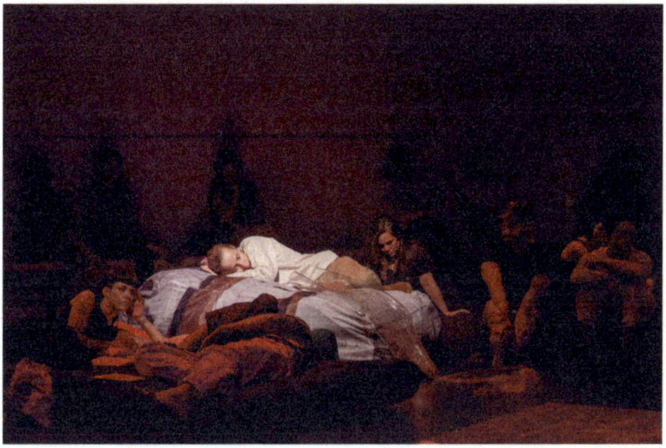

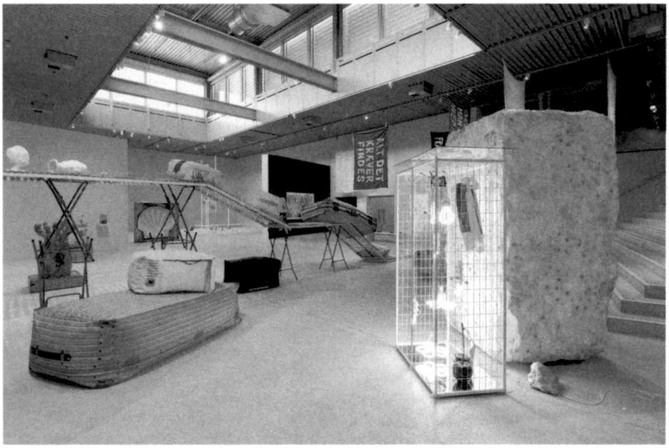
ALT DET
KRÆVER
FINDES

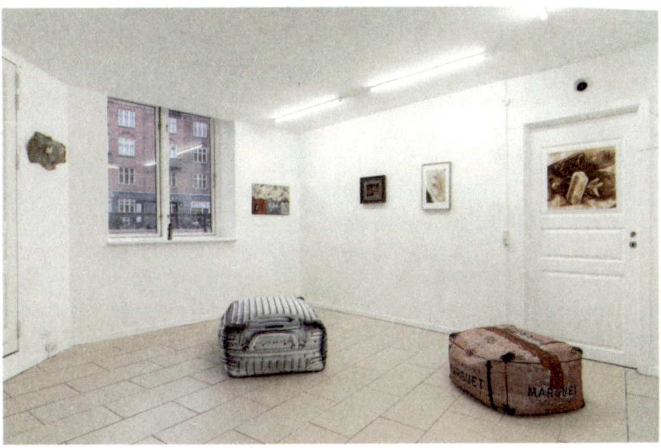
MARGUET
MARGUET

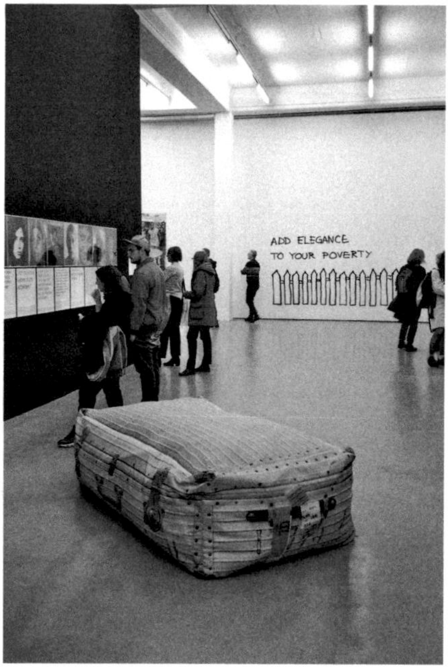
ADD ELEGANCE
TO YOUR POVERTY

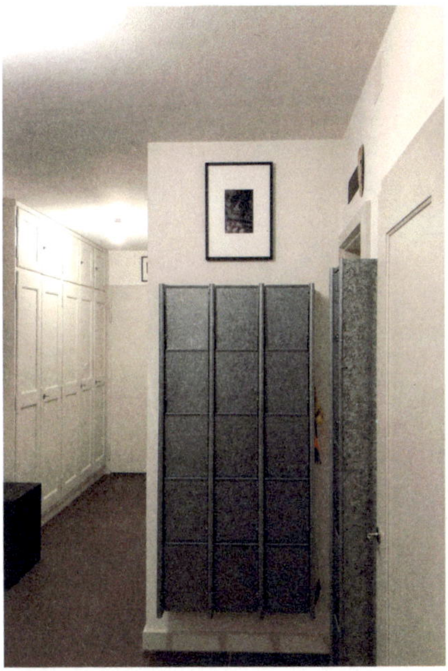

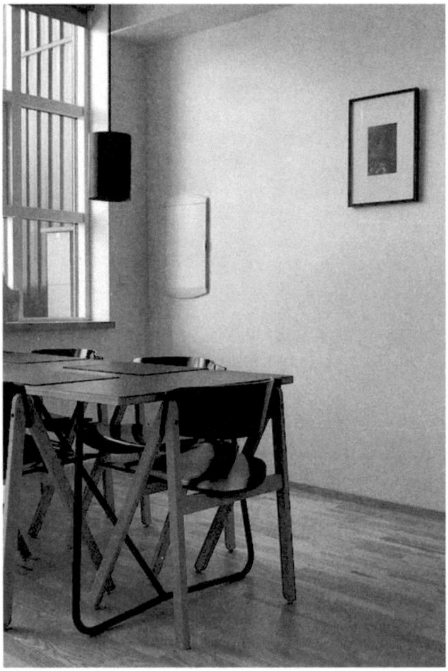

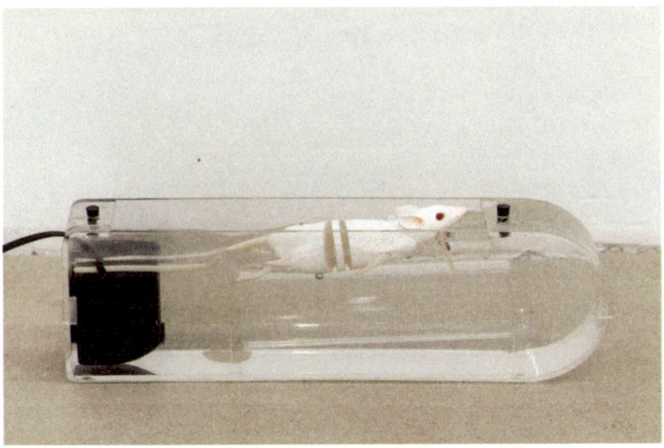

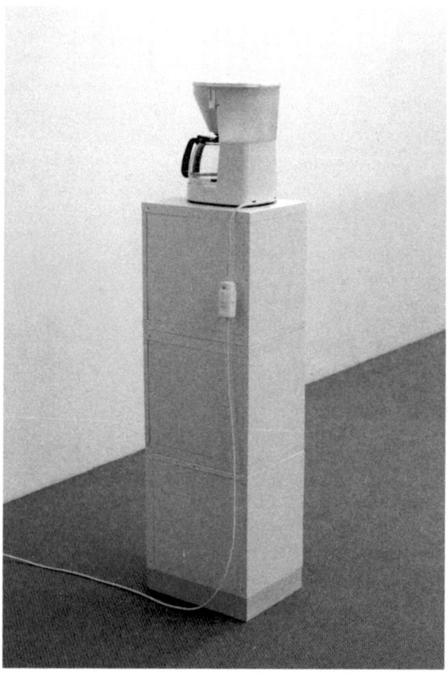

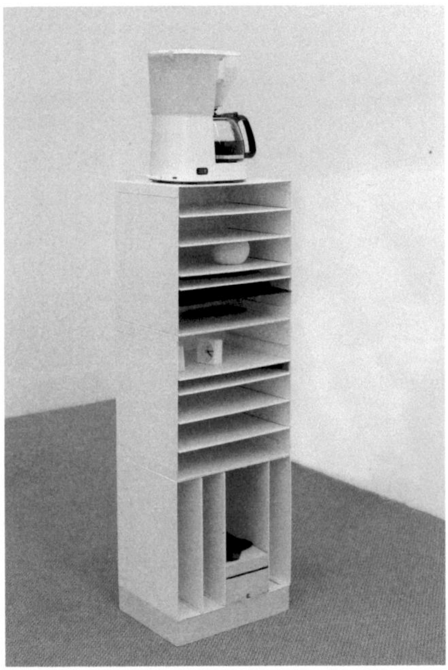

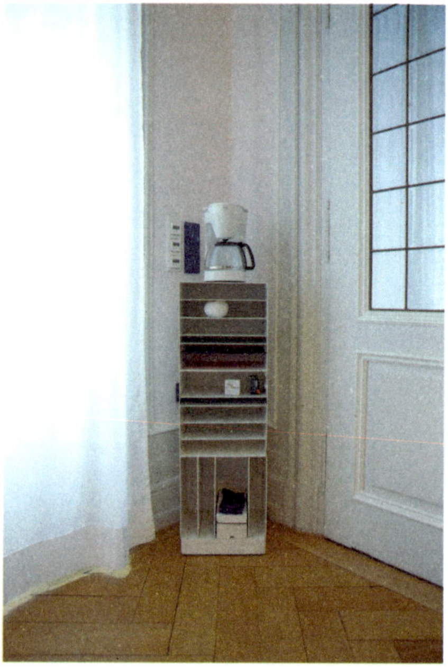

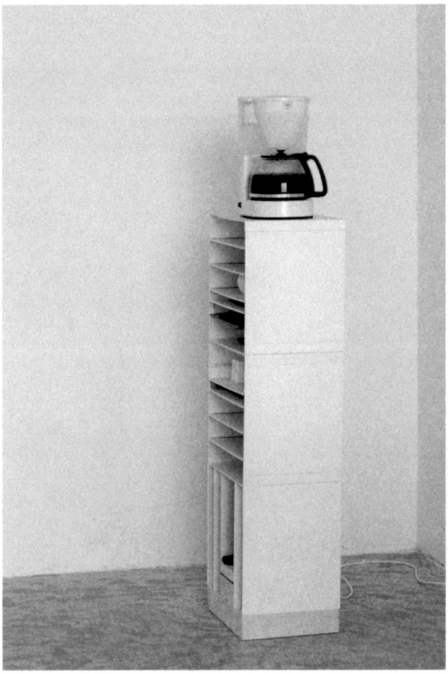

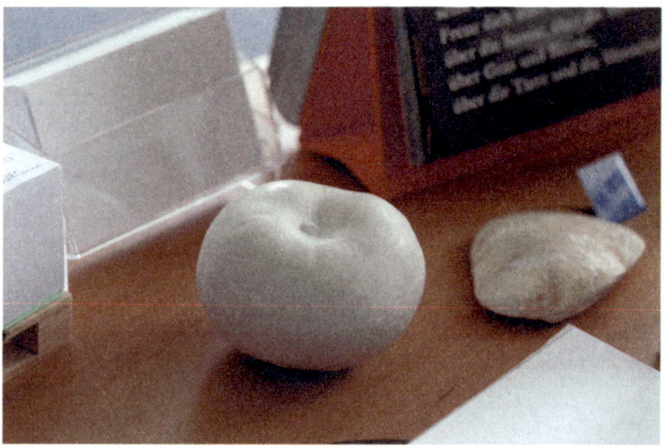

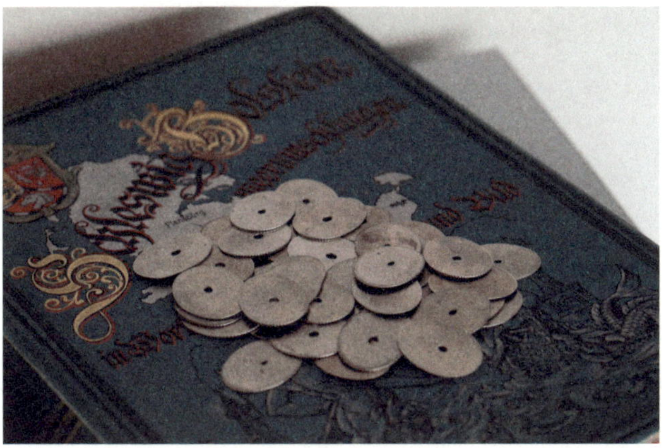

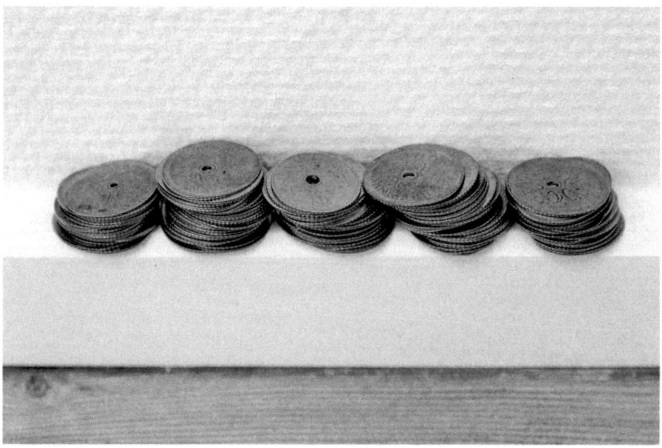

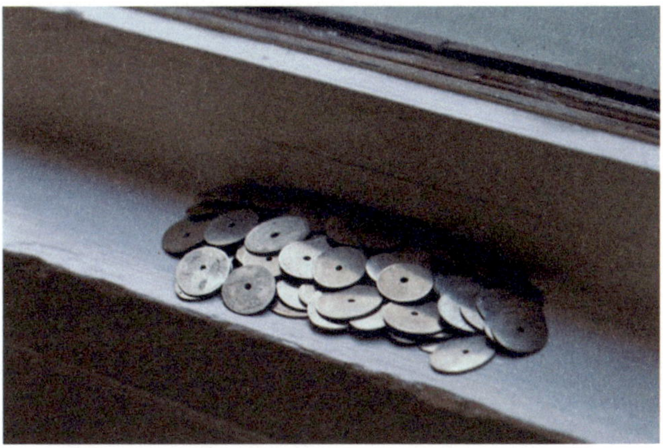

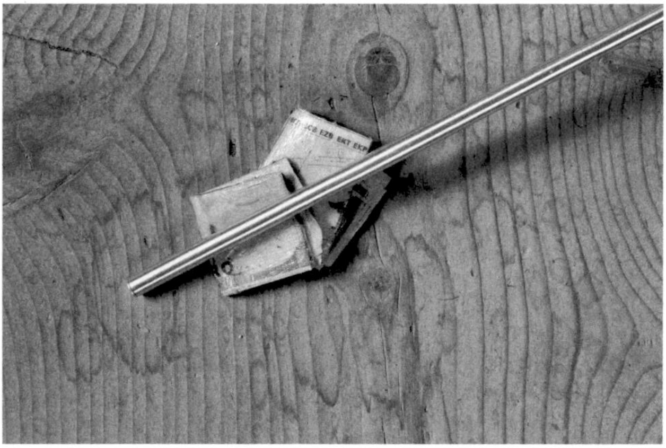

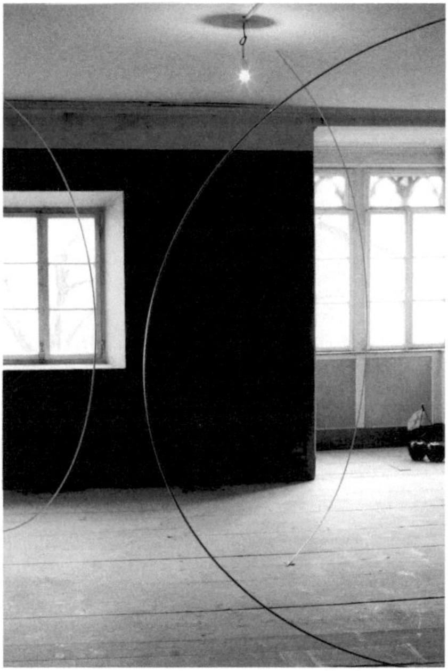

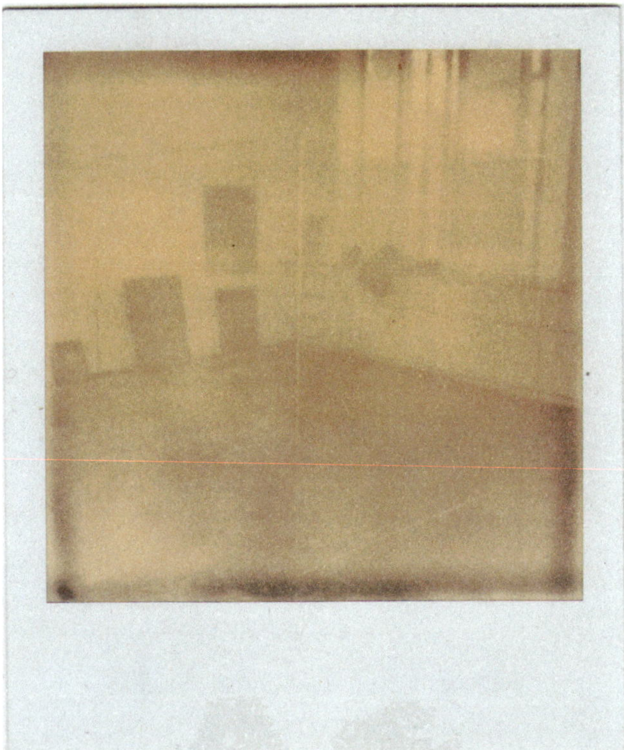

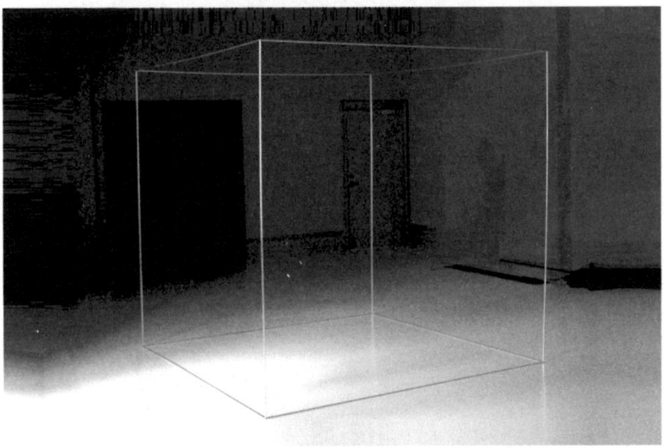

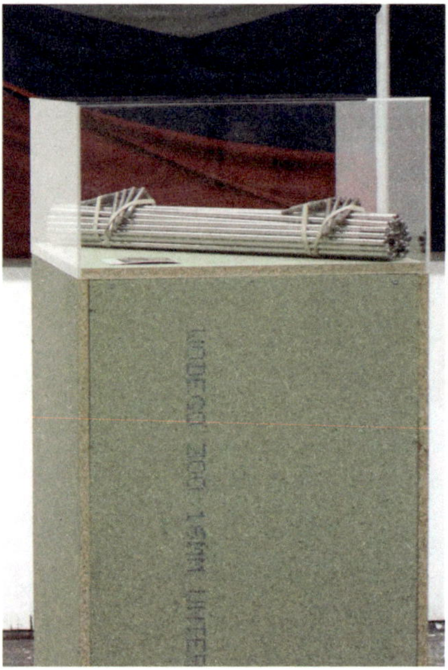

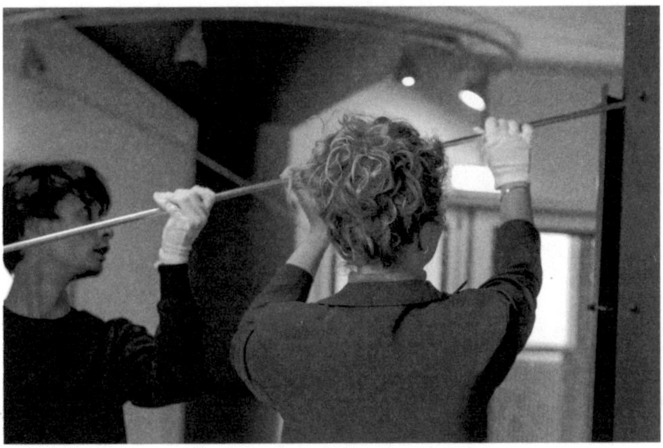

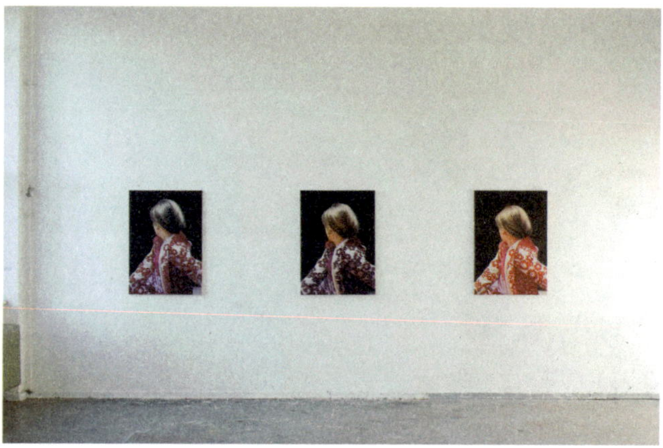

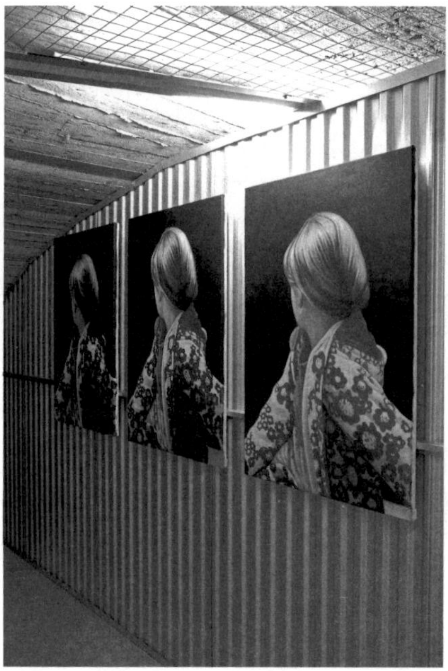

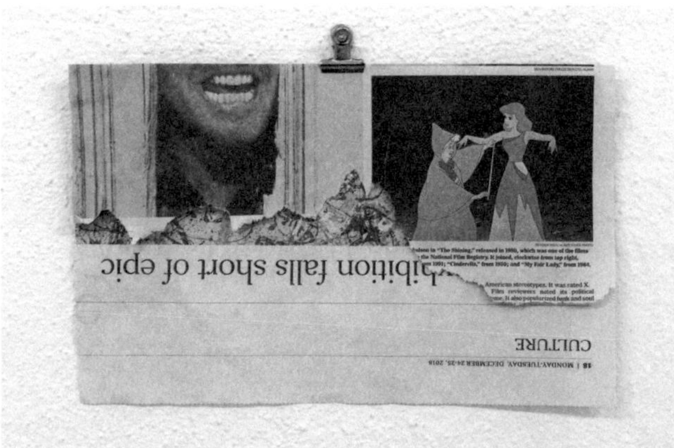
CULTURE

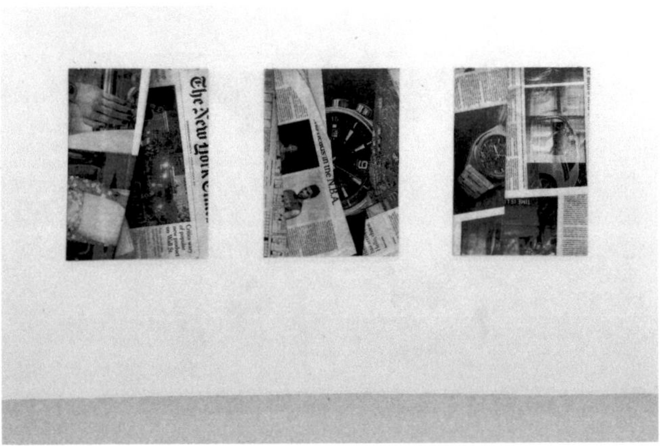

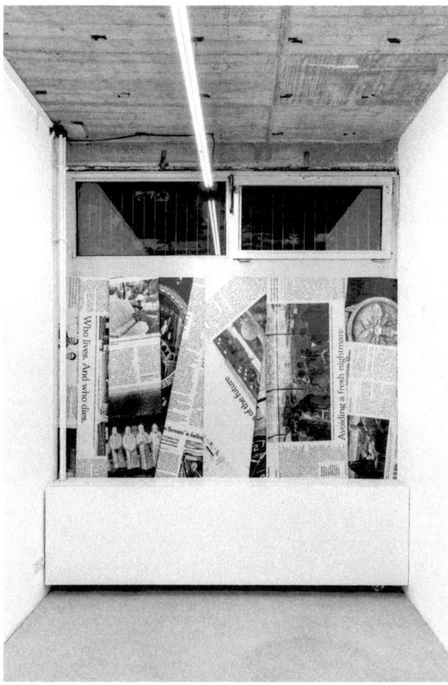
Who lives. And who dies.
of the future
Avoiding a fresh nightmare

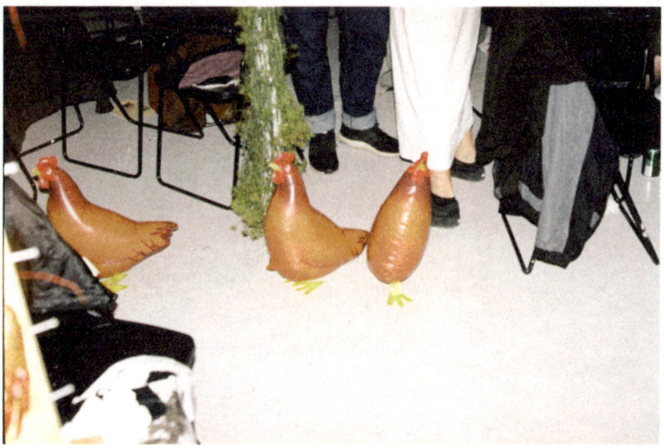

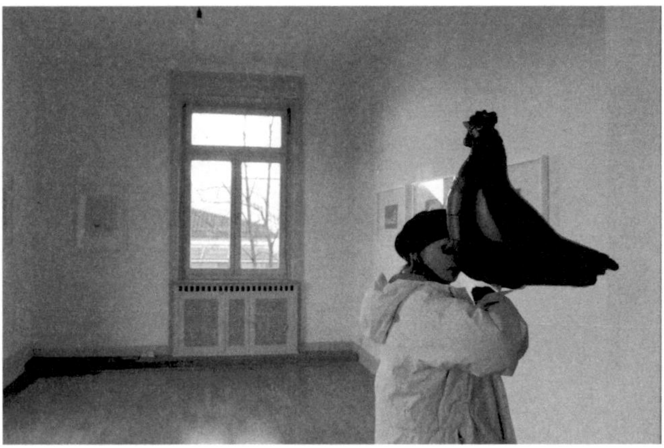

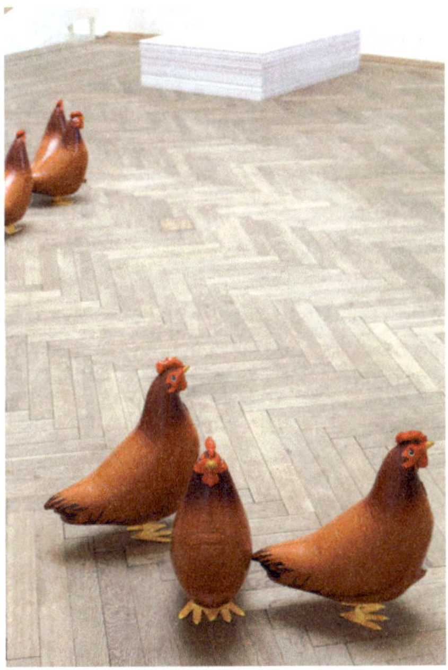

BENEDIKTE BJERRE – A CONVERSATION PIECE

Rhea Dall

STUDIO TIME

Benedikte Bjerre greets me in the doorway when approaching her studio where the sun is apparently always shining. As I enter the atelier for the second time to conduct this conversation with the artist, the temperature has risen about 15 degrees Celsius since my last visit.[1] We've entered early spring. The first time, only a few weeks earlier, the roads were partially covered in snow. Unusual for Denmark, in the unusual year, counting from early 2020 to early 2021; a year in a state of exception, changing rules, new, slower habits, distant viewing, remote access, if any. It all resonates with Bjerre's solo show at Kunstverein Göttingen, which opened (virtually) in the midst of a lockdown (the artist having installed all works via video chat) and, just as importantly, got very close to closing before being accessed by visitors 'IRL'. A show mainly on view remotely, through *reproduction*. A ripe place to start our conversation, as Bjerre sits in front of me, impressive in her stature – even more so than I remember from when our paths crossed previously – crystalline in her wit, dry-lipped, sun-kissed in her black tank top that covers the powerful final stage of her pregnancy. Reproduction.

'It makes total sense and no sense at all, and therefore becomes somewhat bizarre', she comments on the fact that she has made her exhibition a way to revisit and reproduce early work, and that it has now mainly been viewable through another kind of reproduction: the camera's live and still images, conveying the onsite tale of the show. In a matryoshka or Russian doll effect, the exhibition consists mostly of early work that has been reproduced or remade by the artist for this exhibition, only to be, by and large, on display in reproduction. The seemingly outlying operations of remaking and revisiting her works, organising them on archival shelving, as well as recording the presentation through photo and video, thus have become core to the show – this catalogue included.

[1] This article builds mainly on two conversations with Benedikte Bjerre. The first took place on 11 February 2021; the second, from which all quotes are taken, took place on 27 February 2021.

BENEDIKTE BJERRE – A CONVERSATION PIECE

Rhea Dall

ZEIT IM STUDIO

Benedikte Bjerre begrüßt mich an der Tür, als ich ihr Studio besuche, in dem offenbar immer die Sonne scheint. Als ich das Atelier zum zweiten Mal betrete, um dieses Gespräch mit der Künstlerin zu führen, ist die Temperatur seit meinem letzten Besuch um etwa 15 Grad Celsius gestiegen.[1] Der Frühling hat gerade begonnen. Das erste Mal, nur ein paar Wochen vorher, lag auf den Straßen noch Schnee. Ungewöhnlich für Dänemark, im ungewöhnlichen Jahr beginnend Anfang 2020 bis Anfang 2021; ein Jahr im Ausnahmezustand, mit wechselnden Regeln, neuen, langsameren Gewohnheiten, Distant Viewing, Remote-Zugang, wenn überhaupt. All das schwingt in Bjerres Einzelausstellung im Kunstverein Göttingen mit, die inmitten eines Lockdowns (virtuell) eröffnet wurde (die Künstlerin hat alle Werke per Video-Chat installiert), und, ebenso wichtig, kurz vor der Schließung stand, bevor Besucher*innen sie überhaupt aufsuchen konnten. Eine Ausstellung, die vor allem aus der Distanz zu sehen ist, durch *Reproduktion*. Ein idealer Ort, um unser Gespräch zu beginnen, während Bjerre mir gegenübersitzt, beeindruckend in ihrer Statur, sogar noch mehr, als ich es von früheren Begegnungen in Erinnerung habe; kristallklar in ihrem Scharfsinn, mit trockenen Lippen, sonnengeküsst in ihrem schwarzen Tank-Top, das die eindrucksvolle letzte Phase ihrer Schwangerschaft überdeckt. Reproduktion.

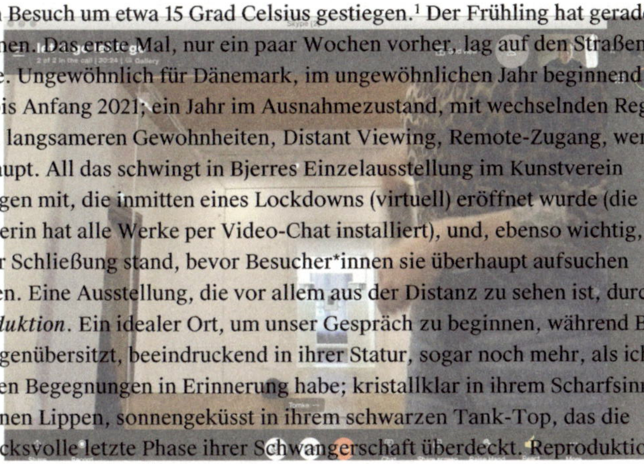

„Es macht total Sinn und überhaupt keinen Sinn und wird deshalb etwas bizarr“, kommentiert sie die Tatsache, dass sie ihre Ausstellung zu einem Mittel gemacht hat, frühe Arbeiten wieder aufzugreifen und zu reproduzieren, und dass sie nun vor allem durch eine weitere Art der Reproduktion zu sehen ist: die Live- und Standbilder der Kamera, die die Geschichte der Ausstellung vor Ort übertragen. Wie bei einer Matrjoschka oder russischen Puppe besteht die Ausstellung hauptsächlich aus früheren Arbeiten, die von der Künstlerin für diese Ausstellung reproduziert oder neu angefertigt wurden, um dann weitestgehend als

[1] Dieser Artikel basiert hauptsächlich auf zwei Gesprächen mit Benedikte Bjerre. Das erste fand am 11. Februar 2021; das zweite, aus dem alle Zitate entnommen wurden, am 27. Februar 2021 statt.

MEMORY PALACE

'I'm usually pretty meticulous working with the floorplan, the dimensions, bodily size, distance. I have a laser-measurer I employ quite a lot, meaning I know the dimensions, the 6.5 metres to that wall and so on. Yet this time the floorplan took up a disproportionally large amount of headspace until very late in the process. I've been almost thinking of the exhibition as a drawing – or online even. From the beginning of creating this exhibition, that's been the process. Somewhat absurd and of course due to Corona, it has been measured out in my head.'

It is circumstantial, of course, that the show was made from afar, in the head, and is its own replica. The context is Covid-19 and, moreover, a stage of life: 'It is also a result of where I am right now with my practice; harbouring a pretty concrete need to turn the tempo down in relation to my own values, evaluate and redefine some processes', Bjerre says. Yet, as with much great work devised within quotidian restraints or worldly matters, the outcome seems entirely meaningful; in this case that the exhibition is constructed almost as a 'memory palace'.

Walking through Bjerre's show – and doing so from afar, seated in front of her in the industrial studio, a former workers' canteen, drinking French press coffee – it is as though undergoing a therapeutic mnemonic choreography in our minds. The process, in turn, reminds me of heralded artist Marcel Duchamp – an influential figure to Bjerre's practice – and in particular the analysis of his ephemeral work in the 2016 publication *The Apparently Marginal Activities of Marcel Duchamp* by Elena Filipovic.[2] Filipovic reads Duchamp's practice through his reproductive, contextual works – in her words, his 'marginal activities' or 'fugitive operations' – that become, in themselves, 'constitutive'.[3] As an example, from the mid-to-late-1930s Duchamp remade his artworks in miniature and collected them in a custom-made suitcase as an edition: his own little pocket survey, *Boîte-en-valise* (1935–41), which he called his 'portable museum'.[4] In creating *Boîte-en-valise*, Duchamp underscored how central archival work is to any artistic practice. He was, to quote Filipovic, 'deeply invested in the praxis of the archive'.[5] Through this archival investment into creating a sense-making narrative or retrospective cohesion in his own practice – independent of where or whether his works had actually been on

---

[2] Elena Filipovic, *The Apparently Marginal Activities of Marcel Duchamp*, MIT Press, Cambridge, MA, 2016.

[3] Filipovic, p.5.

[4] Filipovic, p.114–5. The full title in English is *Box in a Valise* (From or by Marcel Duchamp or Rrose Sélavy).

[5] Filipovic, p.124.

Reproduktion auf dem Display gezeigt zu werden. Die scheinbar nebensächlichen Vorgänge der Neugestaltung und der Wiederaufnahme ihrer Werke, das Anordnen in Archivregalen und das Aufzeichnen der Präsentation durch Foto und Video sind so zum Kernstück der Ausstellung geworden, diesen Katalog eingeschlossen.

GEDÄCHTNISPALAST

„Ich arbeite gewöhnlich ziemlich akribisch mit dem Grundriss, den Abmessungen, der Körpergröße und den Abständen. Ich habe ein Lasermessgerät, das ich recht häufig verwende, also kenne ich die Maße, die 6,5 Meter bis zu dieser Wand und so weiter. Doch dieses Mal hat der Grundriss bis sehr spät unverhältnismäßig viel Platz im Kopf eingenommen. Ich habe mir die Ausstellung fast wie eine Zeichnung vorgestellt – oder sogar als eine Online-Schau. Das gehörte von Anfang an zu dem Entstehungsprozess dieser Ausstellung. Etwas absurd und natürlich durch Corona bedingt, habe ich das Ganze in meinem Kopf ausgemessen.“

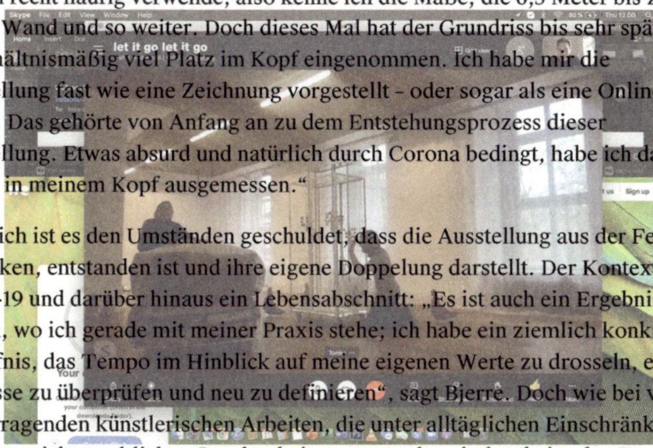

Natürlich ist es den Umständen geschuldet, dass die Ausstellung aus der Ferne, in Gedanken, entstanden ist und ihre eigene Doppelung darstellt. Der Kontext ist Covid-19 und darüber hinaus ein Lebensabschnitt: „Es ist auch ein Ergebnis dessen, wo ich gerade mit meiner Praxis stehe; ich habe ein ziemlich konkretes Bedürfnis, das Tempo im Hinblick auf meine eigenen Werte zu drosseln, einige Prozesse zu überprüfen und neu zu definieren“, sagt Bjerre. Doch wie bei vielen hervorragenden künstlerischen Arbeiten, die unter alltäglichen Einschränkungen oder angesichts weltlicher Gegebenheiten entstanden sind, scheint das Ergebnis überaus bedeutungsvoll zu sein; in diesem Fall ist die Ausstellung fast wie ein „Gedächtnispalast“ aufgebaut.

Dieser Gang durch Bjerres Ausstellung aus der Ferne, während wir gleichzeitig in ihrem Atelier, einer ehemaligen Arbeiterkantine sitzen und Kaffee aus der French Press trinken, ist wie eine therapeutische mnemotechnische Choreografie oder Übung. Dieser Prozess wiederum erinnert mich an den bedeutenden Künstler Marcel Duchamp – eine prägende Figur für Bjerres Praxis – und insbesondere an die Auseinandersetzung mit seinem ephemeren Werk in der 2016 erschienenen Publikation *The Apparently Marginal Activities of Marcel Duchamp* von Elena

public view – Duchamp succeeded in inscribing his early pieces, and most notably his infamous pissoir *Fountain* (1917) into early 20th-century art history, despite this particular readymade being entirely unknown to the public at its time of making.[6]

AN OWN INVENTORY

As a parallel to Duchamp's self-made museum, the portable archival shelving, entitled *Inventory*, placed centrally in Bjerre's exhibition, inscribe themselves into a long history of artists taking over the means of curation, the means of contextualising their own work.

'The first thing you see when you enter the exhibition are these industrial shelves on wheels that carry various artworks of mine, introducing the exhibition's focus or theme of reproduction but also the standstill of time, that lies at its core. In that sense, the shelves reflect my need to stop up and look at my work differently, putting it both into a storage space and into display cases. At the same time, the movable shelves stand freely in the space, creating an architecture within the architecture, even harbouring their own lighting system, independent of the institution surrounding them.'

Visiting the show virtually or in *miniature*, it becomes clear that the entire exhibition functions as an independent index or inventory that, through conveying its own logic and connecting the dots, creates a silver lining that is almost autonomous from its surrounding, institutional logic. Far beyond its physical presence, this exhibition creates a self-fortified narrative of Bjerre's practice. Fortified by the contextual friendships between her artworks, the works can leave their nest and walk into a life of their own.

On the subject of creating a new edition of another work, Bjerre remarks: 'How should this work have been, how should I have made it, so that it can stand on its own and not be dependent on me? This time around I feel they're ready to leave home, where I've always felt they were dependent on me in some way, and all my odd small decisions that only I can reproduce, a sentiment I guess a lot of artists can relate to. This is a question about freedom and the autonomy of the artworks. I wanted to set them free from my presence.'

---

[6] Filipovic, p. 117.

Filipovic.[2] Filipovic liest Duchamps Praxis durch seine reproduktiven, kontextuellen Arbeiten – in ihren Worten, seine „marginal activities“ [marginalen Aktivitäten] oder „fugitive operations“ [flüchtigen Handlungen] –, die in sich selbst „constitutive“ [konstitutiv] werden.[3] Ein Beispiel: Mitte bis Ende der 1930er Jahre produzierte Duchamp seine Kunstwerke in Miniatur und sammelte sie in einem speziell angefertigten Koffer als Edition: seine eigene kleine Taschenausstellung, *Boîte-en-valise* (*Die Schachtel im Koffer*, 1935–41), die er sein „tragbares Museum“ nannte.[4] Indem er *Boîte-en-valise* schuf, unterstrich Duchamp, die zentrale Bedeutung von Archivarbeit für jede künstlerische Praxis. Er war, um Filipovic zu zitieren, „deeply invested in the praxis of the archive“ [zutiefst in die Arbeit des Archivierens investiert].[5] Durch diese archivarischen Bemühungen in die Schaffung einer sinnstiftenden Erzählung oder eines retrospektiven Zusammenhalts in seiner eigenen Praxis – unabhängig davon, wo oder ob seine Werke tatsächlich öffentlich zu sehen waren – gelang es Duchamp, seine frühen Werke und insbesondere sein berüchtigtes Pissoir *Fountain* (1917) in die Kunstgeschichte des frühen 20. Jahrhunderts einzuschreiben, obwohl dieses besondere Readymade der Öffentlichkeit zur Zeit seiner Entstehung völlig unbekannt war.[6]

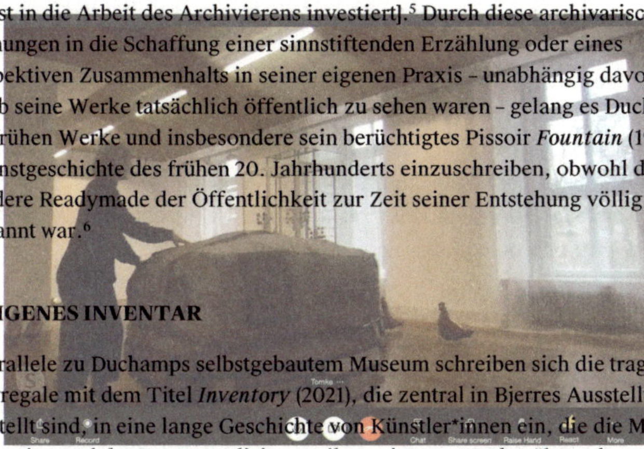

EIN EIGENES INVENTAR

Als Parallele zu Duchamps selbstgebautem Museum schreiben sich die tragbaren Archivregale mit dem Titel *Inventory* (2021), die zentral in Bjerres Ausstellung aufgestellt sind, in eine lange Geschichte von Künstler*innen ein, die die Mittel der Kuration und der Kontextualisierung ihres eigenen Werks, übernehmen.

„Das erste, was du beim Betreten der Ausstellung siehst, sind diese Industrieregale auf Rädern, die verschiedene Kunstwerke von mir tragen und den Schwerpunkt bzw. das Thema der Ausstellung, die Reproduktion, aber auch den Stillstand der Zeit, der ihr zugrunde liegt, einleiten. In diesem Sinne spiegeln die Regale mein Bedürfnis wider, innezuhalten und meine Arbeit anders zu

[2] Elena Filipovic, *The Apparently Marginal Activities of Marcel Duchamp*, MIT Press, Cambridge, MA, 2016.
[3] Filipovic, S.5.
[4] Filipovic, S.114–5. Der vollständige Titel auf Deutsch lautet *Die Schachtel im Koffer* (Von oder durch Marcel Duchamp oder Rrose Sélavy).
[5] Filipovic, S.124.
[6] Filipovic, S. 117.

INFRASTRUCTURAL ILLNESSES

In this gesture of independence lies a question of infrastructure. One might even say a necessity of creating autonomy from the schemes or trenches of the artworld by creating an own system, an own interlaced circulation – the odd sum of pathways that one might even call an artistic practice.

This own institutional creation or infrastructural interest throws us into a discussion about Bjerre's related, background interest in systemic powers, nodding to her own current position teaching at an art academy. She tells her 'origin story' about having first studied sociology in Copenhagen and then photography at an independent pre-college programme prior to beginning her art studies in Frankfurt at the Städelschule. And how, when entering the German art academy, she could not help but wonder why the privilege of being at the master-spangled and merited heights of such art schools was little discussed: 'There was little awareness of which position we were working from, and how intellectualised this position was. As with most academies at the time, the modernist dream was reproduced; it seemed to be taken for granted that this focus was relevant to all others – and that we all knew what was being referenced in these artworks.'

Coming from a place of study where one's vantage point would always first undergo a structural, often Marxist or Bourdieu-inspired analysis, it was difficult to understand why the professors (back then) did not question this elitist artistic tradition more often. These questions led to fundamental enquiries into whether the creative battlefield can ever spur earnest feelings, feel real or be truthful. In this detached bubble of artistic refinery, where did the simulacrum stop and the truthful object or auratic artwork start? Investigating this – with a foothold still in her early photography studies – Bjerre embarked on repeating Gerhard Richter's most famous painting, *Betty*, which she had felt emotionally touched by long before entering any kind of artistic studies. Bjerre delved into the Richter piece (which he, in turn, as is well known, painted from a photographic print of the motif) by ordering three oil-painted reproductions from an art factory in China, long before this such machineries of faux artworks had become a well-known phenomenon: 'These are super early works, built on generally naive questions, about what am I doing here, why is this important. And in this I thought about what the first work was that moved me outside the framework of art, outside being "taught" something is good. I saw this piece [*Betty*] when I was about Betty's age, for the first time.'

betrachten, indem ich sie sowohl in einem Lagerraum als auch in Schaukästen unterbringe. Gleichzeitig stehen die mobilen Regale frei im Raum, schaffen eine Architektur in der Architektur und beherbergen sogar ihr eigenes Beleuchtungssystem, unabhängig von der Institution, die sie umgibt."

Beim Besuch der Ausstellung virtuell oder in Miniaturform, zeigt sich, dass die gesamte Präsentation wie ein unabhängiges Register oder ein Inventar funktioniert, das durch die Vermittlung seiner eigenen Logik und die Verknüpfung der einzelnen Punkte einen Lichtblick schafft, der von der umgebenden, institutionellen Logik beinahe unabhängig ist. Weit über ihre physische Präsenz hinaus schafft diese Ausstellung eine sich selbst stützende Erzählung von Bjerres Praxis. Gestärkt durch die kontextuellen Freundschaften zwischen ihren Kunstwerken, können die Arbeiten ihr Nest verlassen und in ein eigenes Leben hineingehen.

Zur Herstellung einer neuen Fassung einer anderen künstlerischen Arbeit bemerkt Bjerre: „Wie hätte dieses Werk sein sollen, wie hätte ich es machen sollen, damit es für sich selbst stehen kann und nicht von mir abhängig ist? Dieses Mal habe ich das Gefühl, dass sie bereit sind, von zu Hause wegzugehen, wo ich immer das Gefühl hatte, sie seien in irgendeiner Weise von mir abhängig, und von all meinen seltsamen kleinen Entscheidungen, die nur ich nachvollziehen kann – ein Gefühl, das wohl viele Künstler*innen kennen. Das ist eine Frage nach der Freiheit und der Autonomie der Kunstwerke. Ich wollte sie von meiner Anwesenheit befreien."

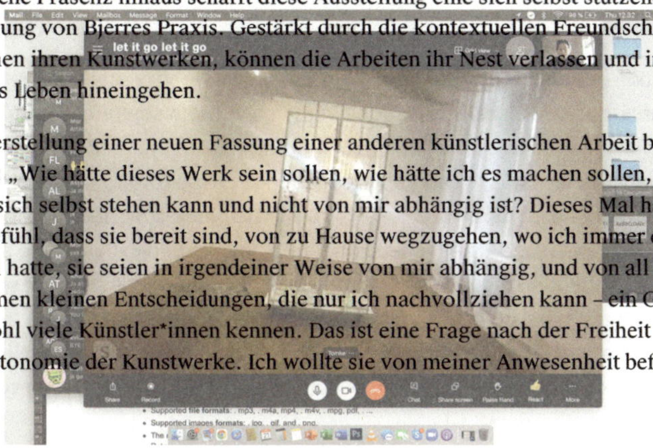

INFRASTRUKTURELLE KRANKHEITEN

Diese Geste der Eigenständigkeit enthält eine Frage der Infrastruktur. Man könnte sogar sagen, dass es eine Notwendigkeit ist, sich von den Schemata oder Gräben der Kunstwelt unabhängig zu machen, indem man ein eigenes System schafft, eine eigene verflochtene Zirkulation – eine merkwürdige Summe von Kreisläufen, die man sogar als künstlerische Praxis bezeichnen könnte.

Dieses eigene institutionelle Schaffen oder infrastrukturelle Interesse wirft uns in eine Diskussion über Bjerres damit verbundenes, im Hintergrund liegendes Interesse an systemischen Kräften, wobei sie auf ihre eigene aktuelle Position als

FROM AESTHETICS TO ETHICS

If *Betty* was originally a work that Bjerre found moving, emanating a certain kind of earnestness, then the veracity was questioned in painted reproductions: 'each had different measurement, white-balance', she explains. Rendered dissimilarly, in varying colours and tones, the reproductions point to the same question: wherein lies the real quality of an artistic output? Bjerre, whose Städelschule studio was the very work space where Richter had taught his classes when he was a professor there in the 1980s (around the time when he painted this exact piece), obviously underscores this play on the question of 'truthfulness' by borrowing the grand male artist's motif. 'Then of course there is a kind of naughtiness in stealing his work', she nods.

The question of theft, copy or replica sends us down a long, spiralling quest of aura and integrity, basic sculptural questions of the carved-out sculpture versus the hollow mould, the façade; and, not least, how this spin is repeated in the show, as Bjerre laughingly remarks, talking about her series of cheap, silly, inflatable, chicken-shaped balloons: 'The chickens from 2016 are hollow, helium-filled tanks – they are a simple façade. The façade is a returning question in this whole array of works, building around the idea of simulacrum, built around questions of what is in fact real, what is a real object, what is a picture of a thing and what is the thing in itself, and what is the relation between the two? That is very relevant in this exhibition, since it becomes a picture of something, that I have not even seen. Wherein lie these borders?'

The idea of a replica is, in itself, an anti-modernist function as it goes against the tale told of a privileged and archaic object that sits at the core of modernist art. Abandoning the modernist nuclear 'thing', Bjerre's work seems to have always been about the (news) stream, the intense flux and accelerated life, drugged up on sugar and coffee, and oil (as Bjerre notes: 'Coffee, just as sugar and oil, is connected to dirty guilt'). Yet while the early 2010s were dominated by a fascination with the fast-paced highlife, there's a different ecological awareness now. As Bjerre remarks, it has been 'a decade moving from aesthetics to ethics'. What was possible in 2010 – in terms of appropriating circulation (of, say, the Richter replicas), travel, transport and production – seems far gone now, in a moment of imploding ecosystems and an ensuing pandemic. If anything, this has pushed at Bjerre's focus on wanting to critically disclose the oddities of life in late

Dozentin an einer Kunsthochschule anspielt. Sie erzählt ihre „Herkunftsgeschichte“, wie sie zunächst Soziologie in Kopenhagen und dann Fotografie in einem unabhängigen Vor-College-Programm studierte, bevor sie ihr Kunststudium in Frankfurt an der Städelschule begann. Und wie sie beim Eintritt in die deutsche Kunstakademie nicht umhinkam, sich zu wundern, wie selten über das Privileg diskutiert wurde, in den gehobenen und verdienstvollen Kreisen solcher Kunstschulen zu sein: „Es gab wenig Bewusstsein dafür, von welcher Position aus wir arbeiteten, und wie intellektualisiert diese war. Wie an den meisten Akademien jener Zeit wurde der Traum der Moderne reproduziert; es schien vorausgesetzt zu sein, der Fokus sei für alle anderen relevant – und dass wir alle wüssten, worauf in diesen Kunstwerken Bezug genommen wird.“

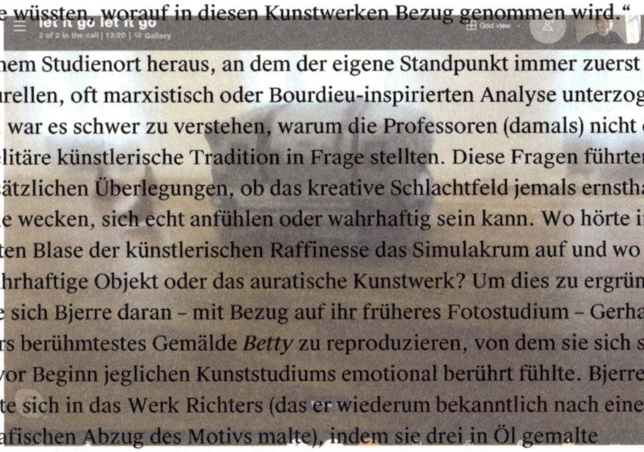

Aus einem Studienort heraus, an dem der eigene Standpunkt immer zuerst einer strukturellen, oft marxistisch oder Bourdieu-inspirierten Analyse unterzogen wurde, war es schwer zu verstehen, warum die Professoren (damals) nicht öfter diese elitäre künstlerische Tradition in Frage stellten. Diese Fragen führten zu grundsätzlichen Überlegungen, ob das kreative Schlachtfeld jemals ernsthafte Gefühle wecken, sich echt anfühlen oder wahrhaftig sein kann. Wo hörte in dieser isolierten Blase der künstlerischen Raffinesse das Simulakrum auf und wo begann das wahrhaftige Objekt oder das auratische Kunstwerk? Um dies zu ergründen, machte sich Bjerre daran – mit Bezug auf ihr früheres Fotostudium – Gerhard Richters berühmtestes Gemälde *Betty* zu reproduzieren, von dem sie sich schon lange vor Beginn jeglichen Kunststudiums emotional berührt fühlte. Bjerre vertiefte sich in das Werk Richters (das er wiederum bekanntlich nach einem fotografischen Abzug des Motivs malte), indem sie drei in Öl gemalte Reproduktionen bei einer Kunstfabrik in China bestellte, lange bevor solche Maschinerien für Fake-Kunstwerke ein bekanntes Phänomen geworden waren: „Das sind super frühe Arbeiten, die auf allgemein naiven Fragen aufbauen, darüber, was ich hier mache, warum das wichtig ist. Und dabei habe ich darüber nachgedacht, was die erste Arbeit war, die mich außerhalb des Kunstbetriebs bewegt hat, außerhalb dessen, dass man mir „beibrachte“, was gut sei. Ich habe dieses Werk [*Betty*] zum ersten Mal gesehen, als ich ungefähr so alt war wie Betty.“

capitalism: 'I've always been incredibly interested in commercials that talk about an object but never in a manner that's direct, truthful. I, on the other hand, have an obsessive craving for the declaration of contents, as in "please just tell me what this is". I'm being super anal about the realness and truthfulness in the work.'

If the early-to-mid-2010s were paced by Bjerre's interest in *Hotproducts* (a piece about candy and shoplifting) and jetting around, then today there's a question of creating a sustainable way of working. Something that holds, what Bjerre returns to again and again, umami: 'In digital production I miss a certain kind of umami, which I think is the best way to describe this, which is a kind of deep taste of tactility.'

SLOW REPRODUCTION

Returning to the reproductions that Duchamp created for this miniature museum, these were, according to Filipovic – at least when considering a readymade such as *Fountain* – far more labour-intensive than the original: 'The process was precise and painstaking, often, paradoxically, requiring more labour than the originals had.'[7]

In the same manner it seems Bjerre's path to this particular exhibition – and maybe more generally to this place in her practice where she intends to 'evaluate and redefine some processes' – has taken her through a labour-intensive reconsideration of her earlier work. In that sense the whole show hits a note about artistic work as reproductive labour: the slowness of repeating, reiterating, rethinking, rerunning, recording. Rather than focusing on creating a singular new piece, it circulates questions of care for the oeuvre or practice. Here I think of care and reproduction, or reproductive labour, in relation to childbirth, nurturing, housework; traditionally unpaid, female responsibilities, as the monumental feminist thinker Silvia Federici would define it.[8] Dusting these artistic fellows off, reproducing or remaking them, Bjerre is believing in the value of her earlier works' continuous productive – and reproductive – function and in the continuity of a practice, instead of abandoning them as standalone pieces and letting them wither in darkness, forgotten in a collector's basement.

---

[7] Filipovic, p.124.

[8] See Federici's collection of essays from the 1970s to the present: Silvia Federici, *Revolution at Point Zero: Housework, Reproduction, and Feminist Struggle*, PM Press, Oakland, 2012.

VON DER ÄSTHETIK ZUR ETHIK

Wenn *Betty* ursprünglich ein Werk war, das Bjerre bewegte und eine bestimmte Art von Ernsthaftigkeit ausstrahlte, dann wurde die Wahrhaftigkeit bei gemalten Reproduktionen hinterfragt: „Jede hatte ein anderes Maß, einen anderen Weißabgleich“, erklärt sie. Die Reproduktionen weisen in unterschiedlichen Farben und Tönen auf dieselbe Frage hin: Worin liegt die wahre Qualität einer künstlerischen Arbeit? Bjerre, deren Atelier an der Städelschule genau der Arbeitsraum war, in dem Richter in den 1980er Jahren als Professor unterrichtet hatte (etwa zu der Zeit, als er genau dieses Werk malte), unterstreicht offensichtlich dieses Spiel mit der Frage nach „Wahrhaftigkeit“, indem sie das Motiv des großen männlichen Künstlers aufgreift. „Dann ist es natürlich eine Art Ungezogenheit, seine Arbeit zu stehlen“, schmunzelt sie.

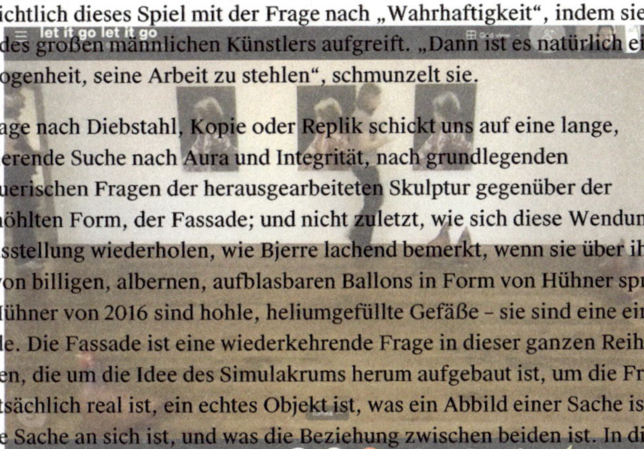

Die Frage nach Diebstahl, Kopie oder Replik schickt uns auf eine lange, zirkulierende Suche nach Aura und Integrität, nach grundlegenden bildhauerischen Fragen der herausgearbeiteten Skulptur gegenüber der ausgehöhlten Form, der Fassade; und nicht zuletzt, wie sich diese Wendungen in der Ausstellung wiederholen, wie Bjerre lachend bemerkt, wenn sie über ihre Serie von billigen, albernen, aufblasbaren Ballons in Form von Hühner spricht: „Die Hühner von 2016 sind hohle, heliumgefüllte Gefäße – sie sind eine einfache Fassade. Die Fassade ist eine wiederkehrende Frage in dieser ganzen Reihe von Arbeiten, die um die Idee des Simulakrums herum aufgebaut ist, um die Fragen, was tatsächlich real ist, ein echtes Objekt ist, was ein Abbild einer Sache ist und was die Sache an sich ist, und was die Beziehung zwischen beiden ist. In dieser Ausstellung ist das sehr relevant, denn sie wird zu einem Bild von etwas, das ich gar nicht gesehen habe. Worin liegen diese Grenzen?“

Die Idee einer Doppelung oder Reproduktion ist an sich eine antimodernistische Funktion, insofern sie der Erzählung eines privilegierten und archaischen Objekts zuwiderläuft, das im Zentrum modernistischer Kunst steht. In Abkehr vom modernistischen nuklearen „Ding“ scheint es in Bjerres Werk immer um den (Nachrichten-) Strom, den intensiven Fluss und das beschleunigte Leben gegangen zu sein, zugedröhnt von Zucker und Kaffee und Öl (wie Bjerre anmerkt: „Kaffee ist, ebenso wie Zucker und Öl, mit schmutziger Schuld verbunden“). Doch während die frühen 2010er Jahre von einer Faszination für das hektische Highlife

As I start moving, jittery from the coffee served, needing to head out, having lost track of time, we end up at *Working Girls in the Age After Reproduction*, two replicas of a sculpture made in 2015, notably both including a (real) coffee machine. The display is thus of a commodity and its double, brewing coffee every day, functioning as – in my reading – two feminist timekeepers of the exhibition, or as Bjerre tells it: 'Having sold my original work, I decided to take it back by recreating it, again, making a new edition and a copy thereof. The two sculptures are clocks ticking, as well as a reference to the film *Working Girl* about what women should overcome. They reflect a general question of the exhibition: what is reproductivity versus productivity?'

geprägt waren, existiert jetzt ein anderes ökologisches Bewusstsein. Wie Bjerre feststellt, war es „ein Jahrzehnt, das sich von der Ästhetik zur Ethik bewegt hat". Was 2010 möglich war - in Bezug auf die Aneignung von Verbreitung (z. B. der Richter-Repliken), Reisen, Transport und Produktion - scheint jetzt, in einem Zeitpunkt implodierender Ökosysteme und einer darauffolgenden Pandemie, weit entfernt zu sein. Wenn überhaupt, dann hat dies Bjerres Interesse an einer kritischen Offenlegung der Eigenheiten des spätkapitalistischen Lebens bestärkt: „Ich habe mich immer sehr für Werbung interessiert, und wie sie über ein Objekt spricht, aber nie auf eine direkte, ehrliche Weise. Ich hingegen habe ein obsessives Verlangen nach der Inhaltserklärung, im Sinne von „bitte sag mir einfach, was das ist". Ich bin super pingelig, was die Echtheit und Wahrhaftigkeit der Arbeit angeht."

Prägte die Zeit Anfang bis Mitte der 2010er Jahre Bjerres Interesse an *Hotproducts* (ein Werk über Süßigkeiten und Ladendiebstahl) und das Herumreisen, so geht es heute darum, eine nachhaltige Arbeitsweise zu schaffen. Eine, die etwas beinhaltet, auf das Bjerre immer wieder zurückkommt, nämlich umami: „In der digitalen Produktion vermisse ich eine bestimmte Art von umami, was meiner Meinung nach der beste Weg ist, dies zu beschreiben, eine Art tiefen Geschmack von Haptik."

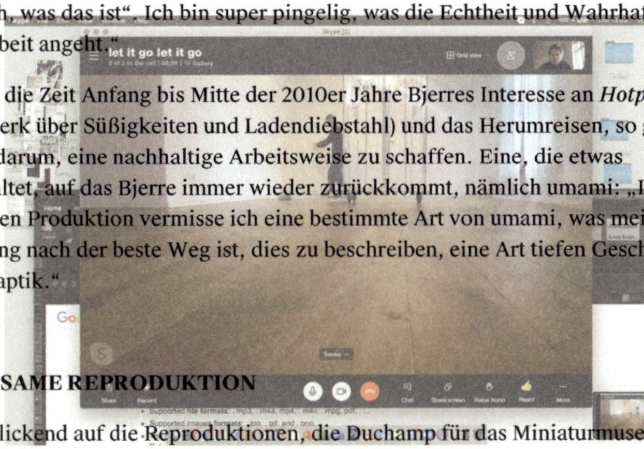

LANGSAME REPRODUKTION

Rückblickend auf die Reproduktionen, die Duchamp für das Miniaturmuseum schuf, waren diese laut Filipovic - zumindest, wenn man ein Readymade wie *Fountain* betrachtet - weitaus arbeitsintensiver als das Original: „The process was precise and painstaking, often, paradoxically, requiring more labour than the originals had" [„Der Prozess war präzise und mühsam, erforderte paradoxerweise oft mehr Arbeit als die Originale hatten."].'[7]

Analog dazu scheint Bjerres Weg zu dieser besonderen Ausstellung - und vielleicht allgemeiner zu diesem Moment in ihrer Praxis, in dem sie beabsichtigt, „einige Prozesse zu überprüfen und neu zu definieren" - sie zu einer

[7] Filipovic, S.124.

arbeitsintensiven Neubetrachtung ihrer früheren Arbeit geführt zu haben. In diesem Sinne bringt die ganze Ausstellung die künstlerische Arbeit als Reproduktionsarbeit auf den Punkt: die Langsamkeit des Wiederholens, Überarbeitens, Überdenkens, Wiederaufnehmens, Aufzeichnens. Anstatt sich auf eine einzige neue Arbeit zu fokussieren, kreist sie um Fragen nach der Pflege des Werks oder der Praxis. Hier denke ich an Pflege und Reproduktion oder Reproduktionsarbeit in Bezug auf Geburt, Fürsorge, Haushaltsarbeit; die traditionell unbezahlte, weibliche Arbeit, wie die große feministische Denkerin Silvia Federici sie definieren würde.[8] Indem sie diese künstlerischen Gefährten abstaubt, sie reproduziert oder neu herstellt, glaubt Bjerre an den Wert der kontinuierlichen produktiven – und reproduktiven – Funktion ihrer früheren Arbeiten und an die Kontinuität einer Praxis, statt sie als Einzelwerke aufzugeben und sie in der Dunkelheit verwelken zu lassen, vergessen im Keller eines Sammlers.

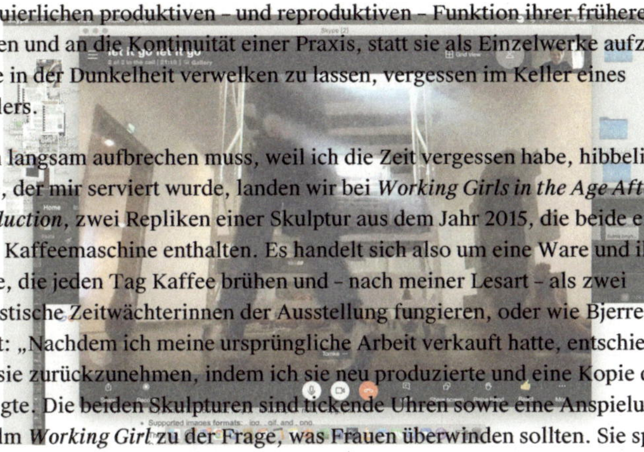

Als ich langsam aufbrechen muss, weil ich die Zeit vergessen habe, hibbelig vom Kaffee, der mir serviert wurde, landen wir bei *Working Girls in the Age After Reproduction*, zwei Repliken einer Skulptur aus dem Jahr 2015, die beide eine (echte) Kaffeemaschine enthalten. Es handelt sich also um eine Ware und ihr Double, die jeden Tag Kaffee brühen und – nach meiner Lesart – als zwei feministische Zeitwächterinnen der Ausstellung fungieren, oder wie Bjerre es erzählt: „Nachdem ich meine ursprüngliche Arbeit verkauft hatte, entschied ich mich, sie zurückzunehmen, indem ich sie neu produzierte und eine Kopie davon anfertigte. Die beiden Skulpturen sind tickende Uhren sowie eine Anspielung auf den Film *Working Girl* zu der Frage, was Frauen überwinden sollten. Sie spiegeln eine allgemeine Thematik der Ausstellung wider: Was ist Reproduktivität im Gegensatz zu Produktivität?“

[8] Siehe Federicis Essaysammlung aus den 1970er Jahre bis heute: *Silvia Federici, Revolution at Point Zero: Hausarbeit, Reproduktion und feministischer Kampf*, Unrast Verlag, Münster, 2021.

MOVEMENT, MOBILITY, COMMODITY

Tomke Braun

Benedikte Bjerre's artistic career began in the 2010s, an era which was defined by rapid speed and high mobility. In the art world, as in other parts of society, a normality established itself that was defined by the fact that a biographical entrenchment in numerous cities became just as much a part of life for many cultural workers as regular trips to major international exhibitions. During this period, Bjerre made the constant flow of services, commodities and meanings, both the starting point and subject of her works and thereby addressed socio-economic conditions. A change in this mental standstill at high speed[1] already became apparent with the increase of climate activism in 2019, and a rethink became eminently clear at the latest with the outbreak of the Corona pandemic one year later. The preparations for Benedikte Bjerre's solo show at Kunstverein Göttingen coincide precisely with that period of noticeable change.

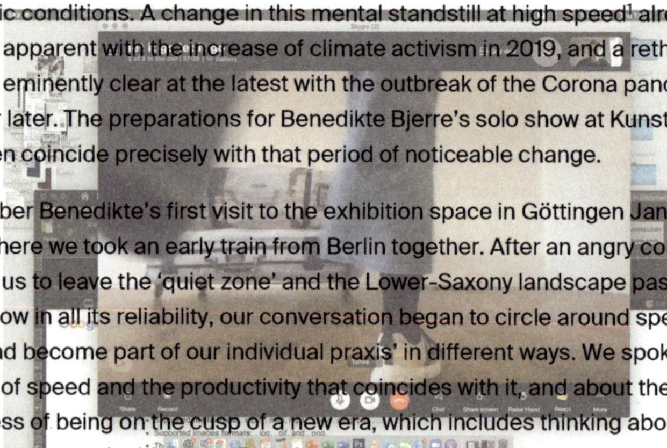

I remember Benedikte's first visit to the exhibition space in Göttingen January 2020, where we took an early train from Berlin together. After an angry commuter had told us to leave the 'quiet zone' and the Lower-Saxony landscape passed by the window in all its reliability, our conversation began to circle around speed, which had become part of our individual praxis' in different ways. We spoke about the thrill of speed and the productivity that coincides with it, and about the awareness of being on the cusp of a new era, which includes thinking about how to work in more sustainable ways. But what does sustainability mean to a sculptor? And what does sustainability mean to Bjerre whose work predominantly consists of industrially produced materials, producing perceptive work about and from within this high-speed capitalism? Following our conversation in the train and the viewing of the space, a first exhibition concept took shape and Benedikte gave it the title *Highways of my Life*. A year later though, following much delay, we managed to set up her show in the midst of a pandemic per video call and decided on a new title: *let it go let it go*.

For her exhibition at Kunstverein Göttingen, Bjerre questions how she can evolve her own practice, thereby examining work-inherent premises of site-specificity,

---

[1] Paul Virilio, *Rasender Stillstand*, Carl Hanser Verlag, München, 1992.

MOVEMENT, MOBILITY, COMMODITY

Tomke Braun

Benedikte Bjerre hat ihre künstlerische Laufbahn in den 2010er Jahren begonnen, in einer Zeit, die von einer rasanten Geschwindigkeit und hohen Mobilität geprägt war. Im Kunstbetrieb sowie in vielen anderen Bereichen der Gesellschaft etablierte sich in diesen Jahren eine Normalität, die sich dadurch auszeichnete, dass die biografische Verwurzelung in vielen verschiedenen Städten ebenso Teil des Lebens vieler Kulturschaffender wurde wie regelmäßige Reisen zu internationalen Großausstellungen. Die dauernden Ströme von Dienstleistungen, Waren und Bedeutungen hat Bjerre in dieser Zeit zugleich zu dem Ausgangspunkt und Gegenstand ihrer Werke gemacht und damit sozio-ökonomische Bedingungen thematisiert. Eine Veränderung dieses gedanklichen Stillstandes bei gleichzeitig hoher Geschwindigkeit[1] bahnte sich bereits mit dem Erstarken klimaaktivistischer Bewegungen 2019 an, und wurde mit Ausbruch der Corona-Pandemie unausweichlich. Die Vorbereitungen von Bjerres Einzelausstellung im Kunstverein Göttingen fallen genau in jenen Zeitraum des spürbaren gesellschaftlichen Wandels.

Ich erinnere mich an Benediktes ersten Besuch der Ausstellungsräume in Göttingen im Januar 2020. Wir sind früh am Morgen gemeinsam mit dem Zug aus Berlin losgefahren. Nachdem wir von einem Pendler aus dem Ruhe-Abteil geschickt worden sind und die niedersächsische Landschaft in ihrer Regelmäßigkeit vor dem Fenster vorbeizog, drehte sich unser Gespräch um Geschwindigkeit, die unseren Praxen auf je unterschiedlicher Art und Weise zu eigen geworden ist. Wir sprachen über den Spaß an der Schnelligkeit und die damit verbundene Produktivität und über das Wissen, dass eine neue Zeit anbricht, die auch bedeutet nachhaltiger zu arbeiten. Aber was bedeutet Nachhaltigkeit für die Arbeit als Bildhauerin? Und was bedeutet Nachhaltigkeit für Bjerre, wenn diese stets industriell produzierte Materialien in ihre Werke einbindet und damit scharfsinnige Werke zu und in einem High-Speed-Kapitalismus produziert? Aus dem Gespräch im Zug und der Besichtigung der Räume ging damals ein erstes Ausstellungskonzept hervor, dass Benedikte *Highways of my Life* nannte. Als wir ihre Ausstellung ein Jahr später mit viel

[1] Paul Virilio, *Rasender Stillstand*, Carl Hanser Verlag, München, 1992.

reproduction and production processes. Instead of developing entirely new productions, she began to reconfigure existing works to concretely alter or recontextualise them. Some works were simply exhibited again after a long period of not being shown, others underwent reconstruction, whereas of some, only fragments were shown. The majority of the works were translated through a modular system into a storage-like state. Even if this approach of deceleration and reflection was meant to describe a turning point in Bjerre's practice, on closer inspection it is just a logical further development. In all her work, she integrates a sociological viewpoint of directly personal surroundings and society in general: If society changes, then the work or viewpoint changes too. Bjerre thus establishes a contemporary approach that, in an idiosyncratic way, manages to combine a view of her past practice with a gaze into an uncertain future.

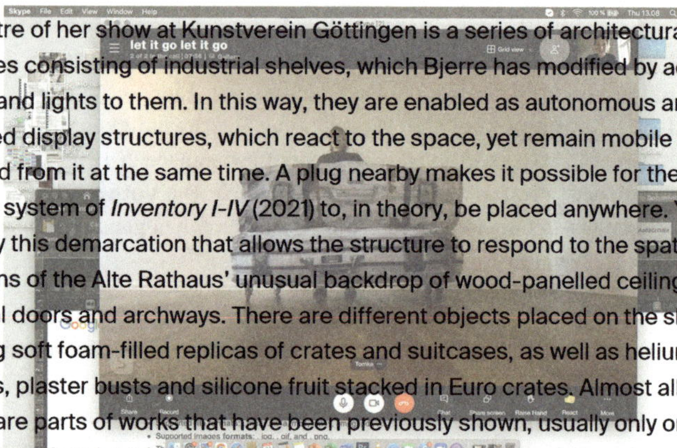

The centre of her show at Kunstverein Göttingen is a series of architectural structures consisting of industrial shelves, which Bjerre has modified by adding casters and lights to them. In this way, they are enabled as autonomous and self-contained display structures, which react to the space, yet remain mobile and detached from it at the same time. A plug nearby makes it possible for the mobile modular system of *Inventory I-IV* (2021) to, in theory, be placed anywhere. Yet, it is precisely this demarcation that allows the structure to respond to the spatial conditions of the Alte Rathaus' unusual backdrop of wood-panelled ceilings, medieval doors and archways. There are different objects placed on the shelves, including soft foam-filled replicas of crates and suitcases, as well as helium-filled chickens, plaster busts and silicone fruit stacked in Euro crates. Almost all the objects are parts of works that have been previously shown, usually only on one occasion, to then be partly sold or the components disappear into a storage space to make way for a new production in the studio. The artworks themselves become part of this flow of goods within Bjerre's own universe of artistic practice: These appear as fragments within the installation, which, on the one hand, act as a kind of index of the artist's oeuvre and, on the other, form a new body of work. The suitcase and crates slouching in the shelves and on casters, are based on objects that Bjerre found lying around in her studio during a residency in Amsterdam. She had fabric printed with blown-up photographs of these objects and then stuffed the subsequent pillows with firm foam. The suitcase, which is repeatedly the subject, is the artist's own and served her in the past for art transportation. The expensive brand-name suitcases by Rimowa are representative of the mobility of a global elite, which jets around the globe for business and pleasure. The scale of *The Rimowas* (2017) transport comfort with Bjerre citing the body-centred scale of

Verzögerung und inmitten einer Pandemie per Video-Call aufbauen konnten, entschieden wir uns für einen neuen Titel: *let it go let it go*.

Für ihre Ausstellung im Kunstverein Göttingen hinterfragt Bjerre wie sie ihre eigene Praxis weiterentwickeln kann und arbeitet sich dabei an werkinhärenten Prämissen von Ortsspezifität, Reproduktion und Produktionsabläufen ab. Statt komplette Neuproduktionen zu entwickeln, begann sie bereits bestehende Werke zu rekonfigurieren, also konkret zu verändern oder neu zu kontextualisieren. Einige Werke wurden schlicht wieder ausgestellt nach einer langen Zeit des Nicht-Zeigens, andere wurden einem Umbau unterzogen, von wieder anderen wurden nur Fragmente gezeigt. Die Mehrheit von ihnen wurde durch ein modulares System in eine lagerähnliche Situation übersetzt. Auch wenn die Herangehensweise der Verlangsamung und der Reflexion einen Wendepunkt in Bjerres Praxis beschreiben sollte, so handelt es sich bei näherem Hinsehen um eine konsequente Weiterentwicklung. In ihren künstlerischen Arbeiten lässt sie stets einen soziologischen Blick auf ihre direkte persönliche Umgebung und die Gesellschaft im Allgemeinen einfließen: Verändert sich die Gesellschaft, dann verändern sich konsequenterweise auch ihre Werke oder der Blick auf diese. Bjerre schafft es damit einen zeitgemäßen Ansatz zu etablieren, der auf eine eigenwillige Art und Weise den Blick auf ihre Praxis aus den vergangenen Jahren mit einem Blick in eine ungewisse Zukunft vereint.

Im Mittelpunkt der Ausstellung im Kunstverein Göttingen steht eine architektonische Struktur aus Industrieregalen, die Bjerre mit Rollen und Lichtern modifizierte. Auf diese Weise wurden sie zu eigenständigen und in sich geschlossenen Display-Strukturen, die zwar auf den Raum reagieren, sich aber trotzdem beweglich und losgelöst von ihm behaupten. Mit einer Steckdose in Reichweite kann das bewegliche modulare System von *Inventory I-IV* (2021) theoretisch überall platziert werden. Nichtsdestotrotz reagiert es gerade durch die Abgrenzung auf die räumlichen Bedingungen im Alten Rathaus, das mit seiner holzgetäfelten Decke und den mittelalterlichen Türen und Torbögen einen eigenwilligen Hintergrund abgibt. Auf den Regalen befinden sich verschiedene Gegenstände, darunter weiche, mit Schaumstoff gefüllte Nachbildungen von Kisten und Koffern sowie mit Helium gefüllte Hühner, Gips-Büsten und Silikon-Obst in Eurokisten. Fast alle Gegenstände stammen aus Arbeiten von Bjerre, die sie an anderen Orten gezeigt hat, meistens nur einmal bevor Teile entweder verkauft worden sind oder die Komponenten ins Lager verschwanden, um im Atelier Platz für die nächste

beanbags and the slouching contrasting with the milieu they are usually associated with.

Particularly noticeable are the balloon chickens filled with helium, which belong to Bjerre's work *Lisa's chickens* from 2016. The balloon figures are based on the comic chickens from the computer game *Farm Life*, which Bjerre uses as readymades. As the already installed exhibition at Kunstverein Göttingen cannot open for many months, Hanna, Emma, Emilia, Mia and Ella are the only visitors of the space during this long period of lockdown. From a distance in Berlin, I would repeatedly imagine how even just a gust of wind could lift them up and (away from prying eyes) they would begin to dance, taking over the exhibition. The work takes on a life of its own, emancipating itself from the artist by being handed over to the air currents of the exhibition space. Bjerre's only intervention in the industrially available product is the naming of the chickens with Germany's most popular girl's names from the year 2020 – initially only visible to the viewer on the bottom of the chicken's feet. It is a subtle reference to another theme that runs through the exhibition, which is reproduction. And not just in an artistic sense, but also on a human level. For Bjerre is herself pregnant during the preparations for the exhibition – a condition that enhances the perceived social change on a personal level too.

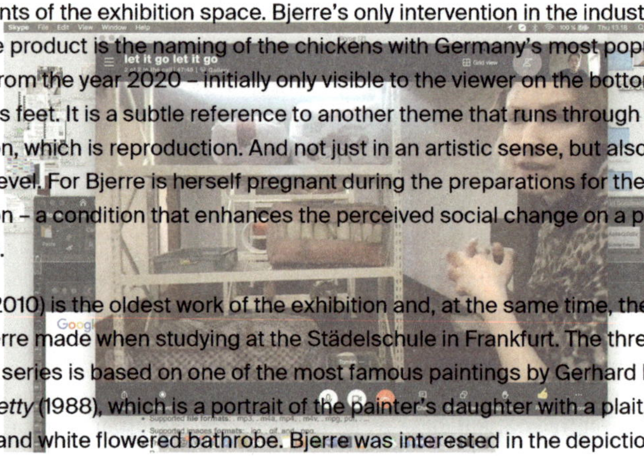

Bettys (2010) is the oldest work of the exhibition and, at the same time, the first work Bjerre made when studying at the Städelschule in Frankfurt. The three-part painting series is based on one of the most famous paintings by Gerhard Richter called *Betty* (1988), which is a portrait of the painter's daughter with a plait, dressed in a red and white flowered bathrobe. Bjerre was interested in the depiction of the girl in which the child turns away, thus eluding the painter's gaze as well as that of her father's, leaving a feeling of discomfort. The original painting is characterised by its blurredness, which is typical for Richter's style of painting at that time. On closer inspection, Bjerre discovered an astonishing fluctuation in the offset prints' colours, dimensions and photographic qualities that were in circulation of the painting at that time. This approach reveals Bjerre's photographically influenced way of thinking and the question of inherent temporality, which also preoccupied Richter when he was painting the picture based on a photograph. Bjerre chose three of these coloured reproductions and commissioned a commercial studio in the Chinese city Shenzhen, which specialised in oil paintings, to produce paintings based on them. The result are three paintings with differing colours, which have utterly lost the blurredness of the original and instead are painted in a style more reminiscent of realistic propaganda paintings. The artist's approach infiltrates the

Produktion zu machen. Die Kunstwerke sind hier selbst Teil eines Warenstroms im Universum von Bjerres künstlerischer Praxis: In der Installation tauchen sie als Fragmente auf, die einerseits als eine Art Index des bisherigen Œuvres der Künstlerin dienen und gleichzeitig gemeinsam ein neues Werk bilden. Die in den Regalen und auf einem Rollbrett gebetteten, fläzenden Koffer und Kisten basieren auf Objekten, die Bjerre, während einer Residency in Amsterdam in und um ihr Atelier herum gefunden hat. Fotografien dieser Gegenstände druckte sie stark vergrößert auf Stoff und füllte die Kissen mit festem Schaumstoff. Der wiederholt abgebildete Koffer gehört der Künstlerin selbst und diente ihr in der Vergangenheit für Kunsttransporte. Die teuren Marken-Koffer von Rimowa stehen stellvertretend als Zeichen für die Mobilität einer globalen Elite, die beruflich wie auch privat durch die Welt fliegt. In ihrer Aufgeblasenheit gewinnen *The Rimowas* (2017) an Gemütlichkeit und Bjerre simuliert das auf Körper ausgerichtete Maß von Sitzsäcken, so dass ihr Fläzen in einem Kontrast zu den mit ihnen assoziiertem Milieu steht.

Besonders auffällig sind die mit Helium gefüllten Ballon-Hühner, die zu Bjerres Werk *Lisa's chickens* von 2016 gehören. Die Ballon-Figuren basieren auf den Comic-Hühnern aus dem Computer-Spiel *Farm Life*, die Bjerre als Readymades verwendet. Da die bereits installierte Ausstellung im Kunstverein Göttingen mehrere Monate nicht eröffnen kann, sind Hanna, Emma, Emilia, Mia und Ella im Lockdown lange Zeit die einzigen Besucherinnen in den Räumen. Aus der Distanz in Berlin dachte ich wiederholt daran, wie ein kleiner Windhauch ihnen bereits Antrieb gibt, sie unbeobachtet durch die Räume tanzen ließ und sie so die Ausstellung für sich eroberten. Das Werk verselbstständigt sich, emanzipiert sich von der Künstlerin, indem es den Luftströmen des Ausstellungsraumes überlassen bleibt. Bjerres einziger Eingriff in das industriell verfügbare Produkt ist die Benennung der Hühner mit Deutschlands beliebtesten Mädchennamen aus dem Jahre 2020 – zunächst nicht sichtbar für die Betrachter*in unter den Füßen der Hühner. Ein stiller Verweis auf ein weiteres Thema, das sich durch die Ausstellung zieht, ist dasjenige der Reproduktion. Und das nicht nur im kunstwissenschaftlichen Sinne, sondern auch im menschlichen. Denn Bjerre ist während der Vorbereitungen der Ausstellung selbst schwanger – ein Zustand, der den gefühlten gesellschaftlichen Wandel für sie auch auf persönlicher Ebene verstärkt.

art world's capitalist production flows that exist independently of her works and makes them her own. The *Bettys* were created very early on in Bjerre's artistic career and are testimony to a change of the artist's critique of capitalism to become a problematic, if not outdated, one. In their book *The New Spirit of Capitalism*[2], Luc Boltanksi and Ève Chiapello highlight the fact that artists' critique of the 20th century's system is already automatically a part of this system.[3] Precisely because of this, Bjerre makes an attempt at a form of counter movement and *hacks herself* into a system to lay bare the underlying structures. Using Richter's iconographic work, Bjerre develops a possible continuation of a system of production and reproduction, making it tangible through viewing her work. The *Bettys* are however not only representative of the artist's early preoccupation with economic cycles and their sociological side effects, but also introduces the theme of offspring and childhood into the exhibition. Significantly, it was the first work that Bjerre can think of that had a lasting impression on her as a teenager. An ambivalent relationship between father and daughter seems to manifest itself in the depicted perspectives and Bjerre, with her almost brazen appropriation of the motif, seems to want to breathe new life into the girl, detached from the gaze and career of her father.

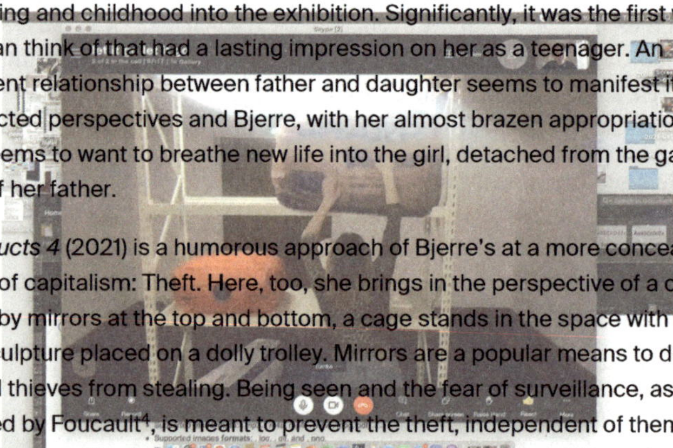

Hotproducts 4 (2021) is a humorous approach of Bjerre's at a more concealed by-product of capitalism: Theft. Here, too, she brings in the perspective of a child. Framed by mirrors at the top and bottom, a cage stands in the space with the entire sculpture placed on a dolly trolley. Mirrors are a popular means to deter potential thieves from stealing. Being seen and the fear of surveillance, as described by Foucault[4], is meant to prevent the theft, independent of them being surveyed or not. The illuminated sculpture is the 4th variation in this series. It is similar to the previous versions in that they are all based on a simple metal grid cabinet, in which a collection of objects and goods are enclosed. Like in *Hotproducts 1* (2015), the variations shown at Kunstverein Göttingen are crisscrossed from top to bottom by shop-display systems with tempting and large colourful lollipops emblazoned in their fixtures. At adult leg height there is a neon green children's bicycle lock, and the key is in it. Mirror and lock are a warning but do not in fact discourage opening the cupboard (in *Hotproducts 3* (2018) the doors were even wide open) or reaching through the bars. Playing with the forbidden, fuels the desire to steal all the more. What fascinates Bjerre about stealing is once

---

[2] Luc Boltanski, Ève Chiapello, *The New Spirit of Capitalism*, UVK, Constance, 2003.

[3] The realisation that art can no longer be separated from the market also shapes other artistic practices of the early 21st century, which are grouped under catchwords such as accelerationism and new materialism.

[4] Cf. Michel Foucault, *Discipline and Punish – The Birth of the Prison*, Pantheon Books, New York, 1977.

Bettys (2010) ist das älteste Werk in der Ausstellung und gleichzeitig das erste Werk von Bjerre, dass während ihres Studiums an der Städelschule in Frankfurt entstanden ist. Die dreiteilige Serie von Malereien basiert auf einem der bekanntesten Gemälde von Gerhard Richter mit dem Titel *Betty* (1988), welches ein Portrait der Tochter des Malers mit geflochtenem Zopf zeigt, gekleidet in einen geblümten rot-weißen Bademantel. Bjerre interessierte sich für die Darstellung des Mädchens, bei der das Kind sich wegdreht und sich somit dem Blick des Malers und dem Blick des Vaters entzieht und ein gewisses Unbehagen hinterlässt. Die ursprüngliche Malerei ist geprägt von einer Unschärfe, die für Richters Malstil aus dieser Zeit typisch ist. Bei näherer Beschäftigung mit dem Werk entdeckte Bjerre, dass die sich im Umlauf befindenden Reproduktionen von Offsetdrucken der Malerei erstaunliche Unterschiede in ihrer Farblichkeit, ihren Maßen und der fotografischen Qualitäten aufweisen. Bei dieser Vorgehensweise macht sich eine fotografisch geprägte Denkweise der Künstlerin bemerkbar und die Frage nach der innewohnenden Zeitlichkeit, die auch Richter bei der Entstehung des Bildes beschäftigte als er es von seiner Fotografie kopierte. Bjerre wählte drei dieser verschiedenfarbigen Reproduktionen aus und beauftragte ein auf die Fertigung von Ölgemälden spezialisiertes kommerzielles Studio in der chinesischen Stadt Shenzhen, Malereien auf deren Grundlage anzufertigen. Das Ergebnis sind drei farblich verschiedene Malereien, die die Unschärfe des Originals gänzlich verloren haben und stattdessen in ihrem Stil eher an realistische Propaganda-Bilder erinnern. Die Künstlerin infiltriert mit ihrer Vorgehensweise die mit der Kunstwelt verbundenen kapitalistischen Produktionsströme, die unabhängig von der Entstehung ihres Werkes existieren und macht sie sich zu eigen. Sehr früh in Bjerres künstlerischer Karriere entstanden, sind die *Bettys* Zeugnis einer Entwicklung, die die Veränderung der Künstler*innenkritik im Kapitalismus als problematisch, wenn nicht sogar überholt betrachtet werden kann. Luc Boltanski und Ève Chiapello haben in ihrem Buch *Der neue Geist des Kapitalismus*[2] hervorgehoben, dass die von Künstler*innen formulierte Kritik am System aus dem 20. Jahrhundert mittlerweile automatisch selbst in dieses Eingebunden ist.[3] Bjerre versucht gerade deswegen eine Gegenbewegung und *hackt sich* in

[2] Luc Boltanski, Ève Chiapello, *The New Spirit of Capitalism*, UVK, Konstanz, 2003.

[3] Die Erkenntnis, dass Kunst und Markt nicht mehr zu trennen sind, prägt auch andere künstlerischen Praktiken des beginnenden 21. Jahrhunderts, die sich unter Schlagwörtern wie dem Akzelerationismus und dem New Materialism gruppieren.

again the social power relations that are reflected in it. Mouth robbery, peccadillo or kleptomania are terms that carry a value and hierarchy. Bjerre's sculptures *Booster (Burberry)* (2016) and *Booster (Plaza)* (2016) elaborate on this. As part of the research, the artist came across a news report in which the police warned of a group using so-called 'booster bags', in which a layer of aluminium foil is placed inside a shopping bag to prevent the alarm from going off. In doing so, they played on the assumptions of those being robbed by using shopping bags from luxury brands, thus deliberately making use of socio-economic attributes as a decoy. Both sculptures comprise of shopping bags filled with plaster, from which aluminium foil peeks out. They look discarded and ridden by rain, the stolen goods already safely stowed away. In both cases, Bjerre was interested in which prejudices and protection measures play into how shoplifting is dealt with and examines the underlying social patterns and structures.

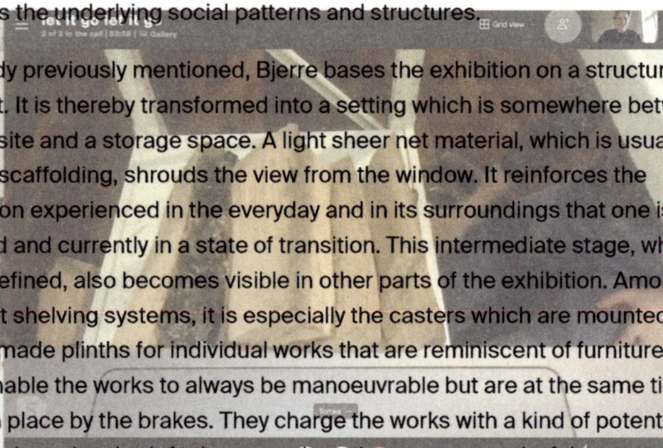

As already previously mentioned, Bjerre bases the exhibition on a structure that defines it. It is thereby transformed into a setting which is somewhere between a building site and a storage space. A light sheer net material, which is usually used to cover scaffolding, shrouds the view from the window. It reinforces the impression experienced in the everyday and in its surroundings that one is detached and currently in a state of transition. This intermediate stage, which is not further defined, also becomes visible in other parts of the exhibition. Amongst the dominant shelving systems, it is especially the casters which are mounted on custom-made plinths for individual works that are reminiscent of furniture casters. These enable the works to always be manoeuvrable but are at the same time locked in place by the brakes. They charge the works with a kind of potentiality that has yet to be unleashed. At the same time, they suggest a playful aspect, which is inherent to many of Bjerre's works. The title of Bjerre's exhibition *let it go let it go* latches onto that and quotes the title song of the Disney film *Frozen*, in which the protagonist Elsa possesses the ability to turn things into ice – or as Bjerre describes it: 'Create sculptures'. Throughout the course of the film, Elsa learns how to make use of her abilities through a series of prohibition, loss of control and withdrawal. It is a story of accepting one's own abilities and personal development, which Bjerre examines as a form of conceptualization of her own skills.

During the repeated change of plans and postponements concerning the exhibition preparations, it felt like a constant *Awareness*-Training: Learning how to let go. The manoeuvrability of the sculptures and their distancing from the space is testimony to this process of letting go, which requires a large amount of flexibility and agility. Equally, the publication at hand can be read as part of this process.

ein System ein, um die zu Grunde liegenden Strukturen aufzuzeigen. Anhand der ikonographischen Arbeit von Richter, entwickelt Bjerre eine mögliche Fortsetzung eines Systems von Produktion und Reproduktion und macht es in der Betrachtung ihres Werks erlebbar. Die *Bettys* stehen allerdings nicht nur repräsentativ für die frühe Beschäftigung der Künstlerin mit Wirtschaftskreisläufen und deren soziologischen Nebenwirkungen, sondern bringen auch ein junges Mädchen als Protagonistin – und damit erneut das Thema Nachwuchs und Kindheit – in die Ausstellung. Bezeichnenderweise ist es das erste Werk gewesen, von dem Bjerre weiß, wie nachhaltig beeindruckt sie als Jugendliche davon gewesen ist. Ein ambivalentes Verhältnis von Vater und Tochter scheint sich in den abgebildeten Blickrichtungen zu manifestieren und Bjerre scheint dem Mädchen durch die fast dreiste Aneignung des Motivs ein Eigenleben zusprechen zu wollen, losgelöst von dem Blick und der Karriere des Vaters.

Hotproducts 4 (2021) ist eine humorvolle Annäherung von Bjerre an eine eher verborgene Nebenerscheinung des Kapitalismus: den Diebstahl. Auch hier bringt sie die Perspektive eines Kindes mit hinein. Von Spiegeln oben und unten eingefasst, steht ein Käfig im Raum, die gesamte Skulptur ist auf einem Rollbrett platziert. Spiegel sind ein gerne genutztes Mittel, um potentielle Dieb*innen vom Stehlen abzuhalten. Beobachtet werden zu können sowie die Angst vor der Überwachung, wie sie bei Foucault[4] beschrieben wird – soll bereits davon abhalten zuzugreifen, unabhängig davon, ob sie tatsächlich beobachtet werden oder nicht. Die beleuchtete Skulptur ist die 4. Variation dieser Serie. Ihr ist mit den vorherigen Versionen gemein, dass sie alle auf einem einfachen Gitter-Schrank basieren, in dem Ansammlungen von Objekten und Waren eingefasst sind. Bei der im Kunstverein Göttingen gezeigten Variante werden sie, wie in *Hotproducts 1* (2015), von unten nach oben durch Display-Systeme aus Ladengeschäften durchkreuzt, in deren Halterungen verführerische und große bunte Lutscher prangern. Auf der Beinhöhe von Erwachsenen ist ein neongrünes Schloss für Kinderfahrräder angebracht. Der Schlüssel steckt. Spiegel und Schloss mahnen zwar, aber halten faktisch nicht davon ab, den Schrank zu öffnen (in *Hotproducts 3* (2018) standen die Türen sogar weit offen) oder mit den Fingern durch die Gitterstäbe zu fassen. Durch das Spiel mit dem Verbotenen wird der Wunsch zuzugreifen noch befeuert. Am Stehlen fasziniert Bjerre einmal mehr die gesellschaftlichen Machtverhältnisse, die sich darin widerspiegeln. Mundraub, Kavaliersdelikt

[4] Vgl. Michel Foucault, *Überwachen und Strafen – Die Geburt des Gefängnisses*, Frankfurt a.M., 1977.

Together with the design collective Åbäke, Bjerre combined a selection of exhibition photos of older works with the pictures of Göttingen, as well as screenshots of the digital exhibition set up. The small-format pictures seem distanced and reflect the (up until that moment in time) mostly digital reception of the works. Texts, like the one at hand, are included as screenshots and are thus made visible as a reproduction of a writing and editing process. An approach which is also clearly visible in Bjerre's work.

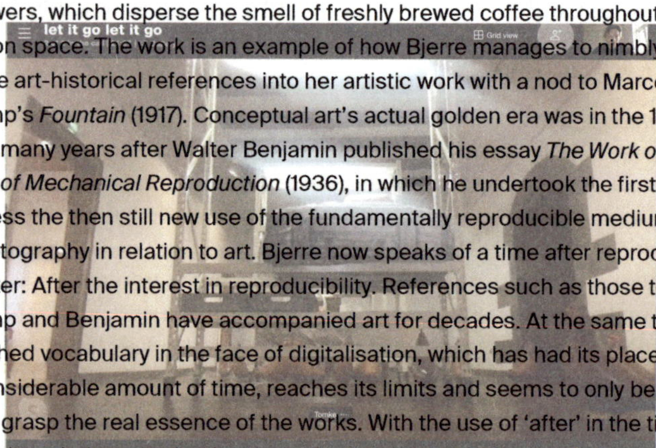

Working Girls in the Age After Reproduction (2021) is made up of two identical towers of filing systems, which are equally synchronized, filled with individual objects: Two plaster casts in the shape of an apple, two pairs of socks, two alarm clocks and a casually folded newspaper. Whirring coffee machines stand atop both towers, which disperse the smell of freshly brewed coffee throughout the exhibition space. The work is an example of how Bjerre manages to nimbly integrate art-historical references into her artistic work with a nod to Marcel Duchamp's *Fountain* (1917). Conceptual art's actual golden era was in the 1960s, so actually many years after Walter Benjamin published his essay *The Work of Art in the Age of Mechanical Reproduction* (1936), in which he undertook the first attempt to address the then still new use of the fundamentally reproducible medium of film and photography in relation to art. Bjerre now speaks of a time after reproducibility – or better: After the interest in reproducibility. References such as those to Duchamp and Benjamin have accompanied art for decades. At the same time, the established vocabulary in the face of digitalisation, which has had its place in art for a considerable amount of time, reaches its limits and seems to only be able to partially grasp the real essence of the works. With the use of 'after' in the title, Bjerre acknowledges modernist ideas of art and reproduction as well as art and productivity, however she also seeks that which is capable of going beyond that. A possible way of looking at this is the influence of 'sampling' and the 'remix' on art as well as other areas of culture, and which are especially widespread in pop music and hip-hop culture. The compilation of already existing audio tracks and songs in music can be similarly applied to artistic methods such as those of Bjerre. Objects, reconfigurations and adaptations can already be found in previous works by the artist. They appear as readymades in constellations with other bespoke objects, whether it is materials or architectural interventions and conditions. Similar to the reproduction of the *Bettys*, Bjerre uses referential systems for herself, lodging herself into and developing work from them. She thereby belongs to a generation of artists that no longer believes in the artistic genius. Instead, she lays the

oder Kleptomanie sind Begriffe, die eine Wertung und Hierarchisierung in sich tragen. Daran schließen auch Bjerres Skulpturen *Booster (Burberry)* (2016) und *Booster (Plaza)* (2016) an. Im Zuge ihrer Recherche stieß die Künstlerin auf eine Meldung, in dem die Polizei vor einer Gruppe warnte, die so genannte „booster bags" benutzten, bei denen eine Schicht Alufolie im Inneren einer Einkaufstüte angebracht ist, um das Losgehen des Alarms zu verhindern. Sie spielten dabei mit den Annahmen der Bestohlenen, indem sie Einkaufstaschen von Luxusmarken verwendeten und somit sozio-ökonomische Kennzeichen bewusst zur Täuschung einsetzten. Die beiden Skulpturen bestehen aus mit Gips gefüllten Einkaufstaschen, aus denen die Alufolie vereinzelt hervorblinkt. Sie sehen aus wie zur Seite geworfen und vom Regen verschlissen, die Diebesbeute bereits in Sicherheit gebracht. Bjerre interessierte in beiden Fällen, welche Vorurteile und Schutzmechanismen in den Umgang mit Ladendiebstahl hineinspielen und untersucht die zugrunde liegenden sozialen Muster und Strukturen.

Wie bereits erwähnt, legt Bjerre der Ausstellung eine sie prägende Struktur zugrunde. Dadurch wird diese in ein Setting zwischen Baustelle und Lager verwandelt. Ein leichter weißer Netzstoff, der üblicherweise als Verkleidung für Baugerüste verwendet wird, verschleiert den Blick aus dem Fenster. Er verstärkt den Eindruck aus dem Alltag und der Umgebung entrückt zu sein und sich in einem Übergangszustand zu befinden. Dieser Zwischenzustand, der nicht weiter definiert ist, macht sich auch in anderen Bereichen der Ausstellung bemerkbar. Innerhalb des dominierenden Regalsystems sind es insbesondere die Rollen, die ihrerseits unter maßgefertigten Podesten für einzelne Werke angebracht sind, sodass sie an Möbelroller erinnern. Durch sie bleiben die Werke theoretisch beweglich, sind jedoch zugleich durch die Bremsen arretiert. Sie laden die Werke mit einer Potentialität auf, die sich noch nicht entfaltet hat. Gleichzeitig zeigen sie einen spielerischen Aspekt, der in vielen von Bjerres Werken enthalten ist. Der Titel der Ausstellung von Bjerre *let it go let it go* schließt daran an und zitiert den Titelsong des Disney-Films *Frozen*, in dem die Protagonistin Elsa seit ihrer Geburt die Fähigkeit besitzt Dinge in Eis zu verwandeln – oder wie Bjerre es beschreibt, „Skulpturen zu erschaffen". Im Laufe des Films lernt Elsa zwischen Verboten, Kontrollverlust und Rückzug den Umgang mit ihren Fähigkeiten. Eine Geschichte der Akzeptanz der eigenen Fähigkeiten und der persönlichen Entwicklung, Bjerre für die Konzeptualisierung der eigenen Kräfte nachspürt.

methods of production, reproduction and circulation bare and, precisely for this reason, gives rise to something new.

The exhibition in Göttingen ends with *JIT* (2021), in which one of the shelves also functions as a barrier into the next room. Her photograph *Vanitas Stilleven* (2016) is mounted on a bar at eye level and borrows from classical vanitas still lifes with objects such as the skull, a skeleton hand (both plastic) and garlic cloves. In the upper righthand corner, one can see a neon yellow label, which ruptures the typical muted colours of vanitas. The ephemerality of the motif stands in stark contrast to the barely degradable and thus non-ephemeral plastic net – a symbol of waste and a further processing of capitalism in her practice (such as the shoplifting or the outsourcing of production to China). The title *JIT* is an abbreviation of just-in-time production, preventing over-production and minimising storage. The artist places the existential motif of the vanitas still lifes in relation to a progressive way of production, which could herald a lasting change in capitalism as we know it. However, it is a way of thinking that sounds ironic when it is reapplied to the artistic practice and leads back to the initial question of how a sustainable artist's practice can look like.

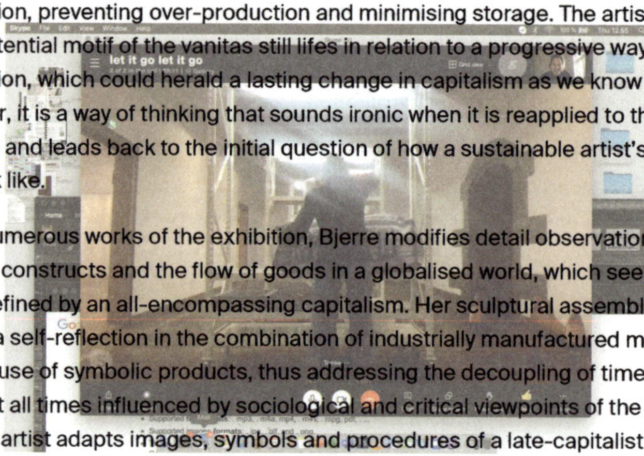

In the numerous works of the exhibition, Bjerre modifies detail observations of societal constructs and the flow of goods in a globalised world, which seem yet again defined by an all-encompassing capitalism. Her sculptural assemblages display a self-reflection in the combination of industrially manufactured materials and the use of symbolic products, thus addressing the decoupling of time and place. At all times influenced by sociological and critical viewpoints of the present day, the artist adapts images, symbols and procedures of a late-capitalist commodity world. By reframing her own works with a display system, Bjerre takes a step back in order to look forward. Metaphorically speaking, she places a question mark above her works, so, above her own production and role in society. In doing so, she makes a contribution to the search for developing the current discourse and making a change in society feasible.

Als im Zuge der Vorbereitungen zur Ausstellung viele Dinge wiederholt verworfen und umgeplant worden sind, fühlte es sich wie ein ständiges *Awareness*-Training an: sich darin einüben loszulassen. Die Beweglichkeit in den Skulpturen und ihre Distanzierung zu den Räumlichkeiten ist Zeugnis von diesem Prozess des Loslassens, der ein erhöhtes Maß an Flexibilität und Agilität erfordert. Auch die vorliegende Publikation kann als Teil dieses Prozesses gelesen werden. Gemeinsam mit dem Design-Kollektiv Åbäke hat Bjerre eine Auswahl von Ausstellungsfotos älterer Werke mit den Ansichten aus Göttingen, aber auch Screenshots von dem digital stattfindenden Aufbauprozess verbunden. Die kleinformatigen Abbildungen wirken distanziert und reflektieren die bis dahin vor allem digitale Rezeption der Werke. Texte wie der vorliegende werden als Screenshot eingebunden und somit als Reproduktion eines Schreib- und Lektoratsprozesses sichtbar gemacht. Ein Vorgehen, das auch in Bjerres Arbeiten sichtbar ist.

Working Girls in the Age After Reproduction (2021) besteht aus zwei identischen Türmen aus Aktenablagesystemen, die ebenso synchron mit einzelnen Objekten gefüllt sind: Zwei Gipsgüsse in Form eines Apfels, zwei Paar Socken, zwei Wecker und jeweils eine legere zusammengefaltete Zeitung. Auf den beiden Türmen steht eine surrende Kaffeemaschine, die den Duft von frisch gebrühtem Kaffee in den Ausstellungsräumen verbreitet. Das Werk ist ein Beispiel dafür, wie Bjerre leichtfüßig kunsthistorische Referenzen in ihre künstlerischen Arbeiten einarbeitet, wenn sie mit den Kaffeemaschinen einen Bezug zu Marcel Duchamps Readymade *Fountain* (1917) herstellt. Die Konzeptkunst als solche hat erst in den 1960er Jahren ihr eigentliches Hoch erlebt, also viele Jahre nachdem Walter Benjamin seinen Aufsatz *Das Kunstwerk im Zeitalter seiner technischen Reproduzierbarkeit* (1936) veröffentlichte und darin den ersten Versuch unternahm, die damals noch neue Verwendung von den grundsätzlich reproduzierbaren Medien Film und Fotografie in Bezug auf die Kunst zu theoretisieren. Bjerre spricht nun von einer Zeit nach der Reproduzierbarkeit – oder vielleicht besser: nach dem Interesse an der Reproduzierbarkeit. Referenzen wie jene zu Duchamp und Benjamin begleiten die Kunst bereits seit Jahrzehnten. Gleichzeitig gelangt das etablierte Vokabular angesichts der Digitalisierung, die sich längst auch in der Kunst wiederfindet, an ihre Grenzen und scheint nur noch teilweise den Kern der Werke erfassen zu können. Mit dem „Nach“ im Titel erkennt Bjerre modernistische Ideen von Kunst und Reproduktion sowie Kunst und Produktivität zwar an, sucht jedoch gleichzeitig nach dem, was darüber

hinauszugehen vermag. Eine mögliche Sichtweise ist die Prägung der Kunst wie auch andere Kulturbereiche durch das „Sampling" und den „Remix", die sich besonders in der Popmusik und Hip-Hop Kultur großer Beliebtheit erfreuten. Das Zusammensetzen von bereits existierenden Audiospuren und Songs in der Musik lässt sich ähnlich auf die künstlerischen Arbeitsweisen wie jene von Bjerre anwenden. In den Werken der Künstlerin finden sich stets bereits existierende Gegenstände oder Rekonfigurationen und Adaptionen dieser wieder. Als Readymades treten sie in Konstellationen mit anderen, eigens angefertigten Gegenständen auf, seien es Materialien oder architektonische Interventionen und Gegebenheiten. Ähnlich wie bei den Reproduktionen der *Bettys*, nutzt Bjerre Referenzsysteme für sich, nistet sich darin ein und entwickelt daraus ihre Werke. Sie gehört damit zu einer Generation von Künstler*innen, die nicht mehr an dem Ideal des künstlerischen Genies festhalten. Stattdessen legen Sie die Formen der Produktion, Reproduktion und Zirkulation frei und bringen gerade deshalb Neues hervor.

Die Ausstellung in Göttingen endet mit *JIT* (2021), bei dem eines der Regale gleichzeitig als eine Sperre in den nächsten Raum fungiert. An eine auf Augenhöhe angebrachte Strebe ist Bjerres Fotografie *Vanitas Stilleven* (2016) montiert, die angelehnt an klassische Vanitas-Stillleben Gegenstände wie einen Totenkopf, eine Skelett-Hand (beides aus Plastik) und Knoblauchzehen zeigt. Im oberen rechten Eck erkennt man ein neongelbes Etikett, welches die für Vanitas ebenso üblichen gedeckten Farben aufbricht. Die Vergänglichkeit im Motiv steht in starkem Kontrast zu dem kaum abbaubaren und somit nicht vergänglichen Plastik-Netz – ein Symbol des Abfalls und eine weitere Verarbeitung des Kapitalismus in ihrer Praxis (wie der Ladendiebstahl oder die Auslagerung einer Produktion nach China). Der Titel *JIT* ist die Abkürzung für Just-in-time-Produktion, die Überproduktion verhindern und Lagerraum minimieren soll. Das existentielle Motiv des Vanitas-Stilllebens stellt die Künstlerin hier in Bezug zu einer zukunftsweisenden Produktionsweise, die eine nachhaltige Veränderung des Kapitalismus, wie wir ihn heute kennen, einläuten könnte. Eine Denkweise, die allerdings einen ironischen Ton bekommt, wenn sie auf künstlerische Praktiken umgedeutet wird und zurück zur eingangs gestellter Frage führt wie eine nachhaltige Praxis als Künstlerin aussehen kann.

In den verschiedenen Werken der Ausstellung wandelt Bjerre Detail-Beobachtungen der gesellschaftlichen Konstrukte und der Warenströme in einer globalisierten Welt ab, die einmal mehr geprägt zu sein scheint von

einem allumfassenden Kapitalismus. Ihre skulpturalen Assemblagen zeigen ein Selbstverständnis in der Kombination von industriell gefertigten Materialien und dem Aufgreifen von symbolkräftigen Produkten, um damit die zunehmende Entkoppelung von Zeit und Raum zu thematisieren. Stets geprägt durch einen soziologischen und kritischen Blick auf die Gegenwart, adaptiert die Künstlerin Bilder, Zeichen und Verfahrensweisen einer spätkapitalistischen Warenwelt. Mit der Neurahmung ihrer eigenen Werke in einem Display-System geht Bjerre jedoch einen Schritt zurück, um nach vorne blicken zu können. Sie setzt metaphorisch gesprochen ein Fragezeichen hinter ihre Werke, also hinter ihre eigene Produktion und Rolle in der Gesellschaft. Damit leistet sie einen Beitrag zu der Suche danach, wie eine Weiterentwicklung der bestehenden Diskurse und damit ein gesellschaftlicher Wandel möglich sind.

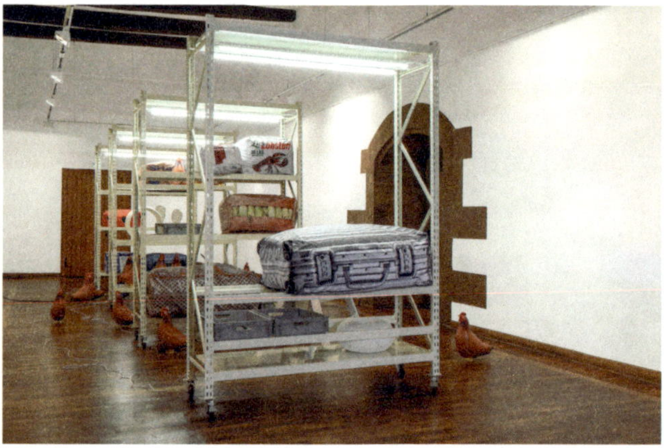

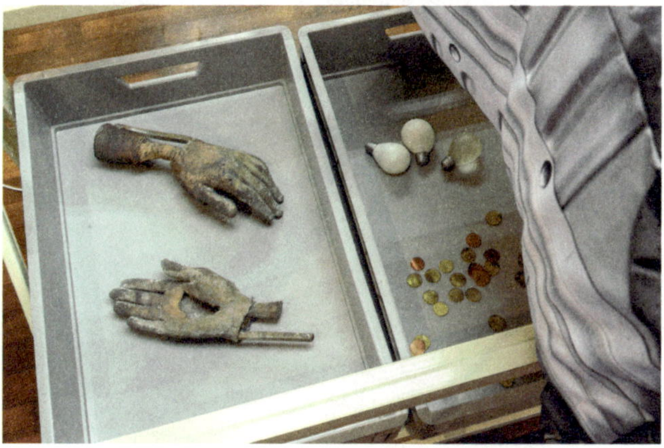

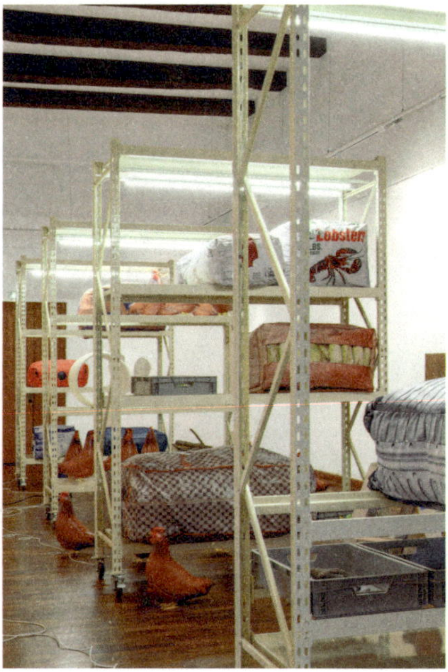
Lobster

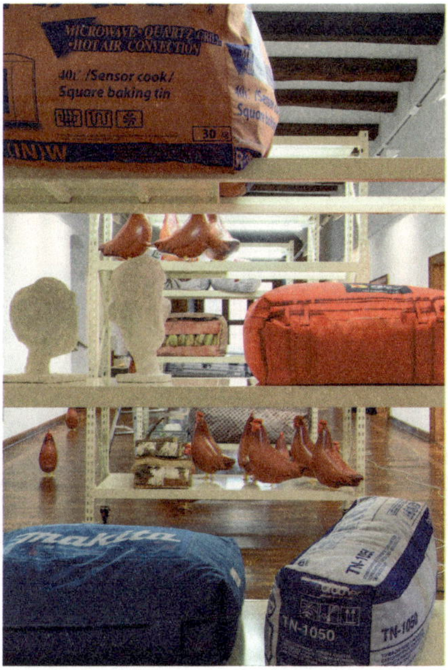
/Sensor cook/
Square baking tin
makita
TN-1050
TN-1050

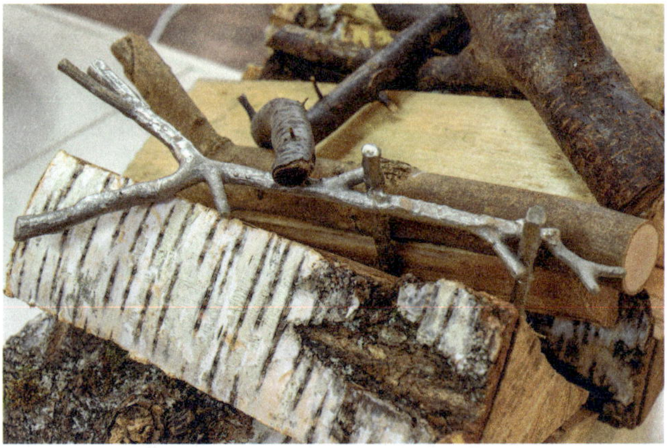

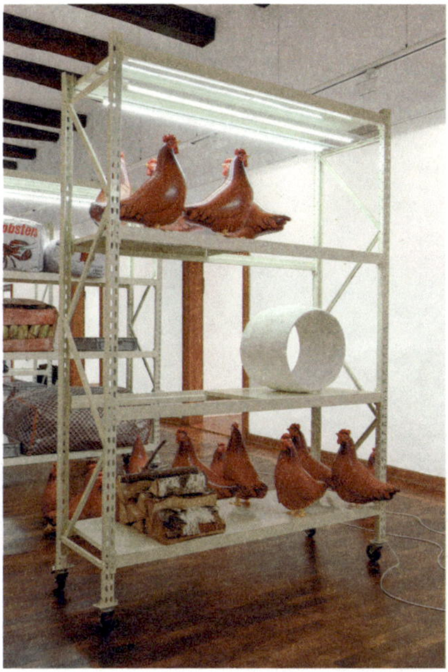

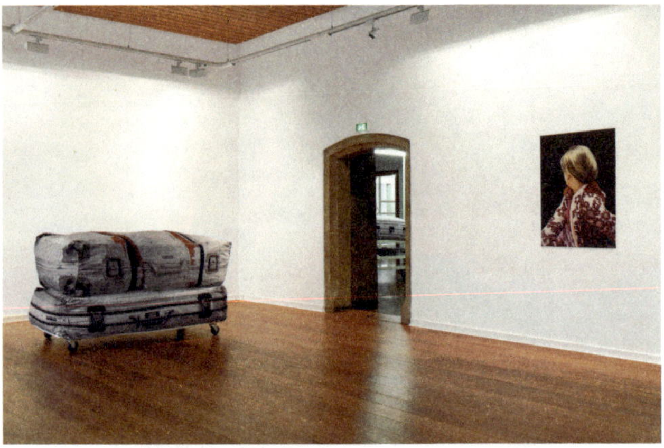

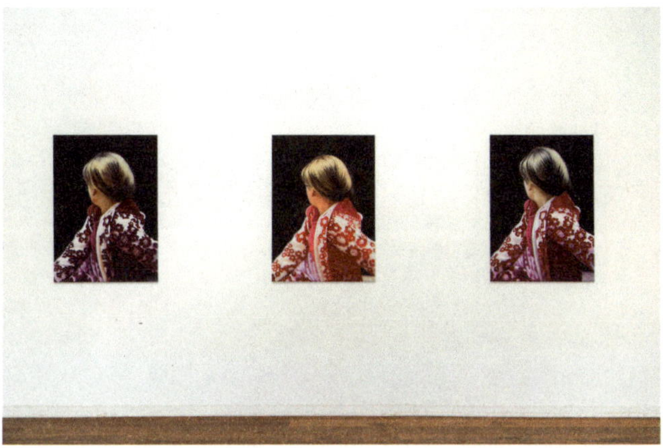

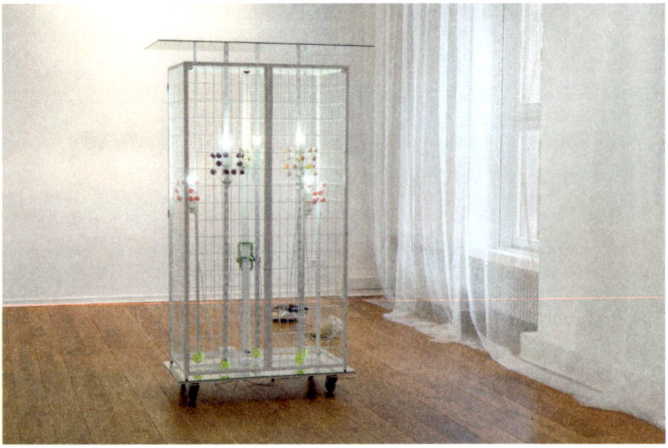

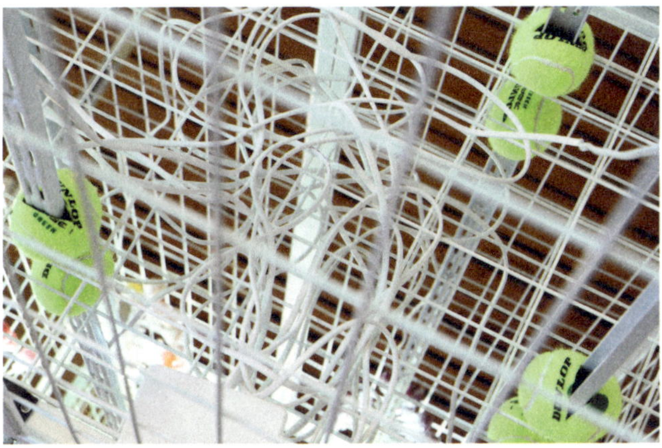

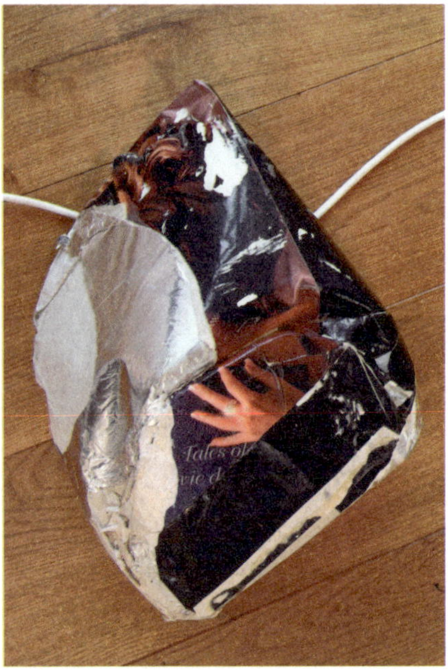

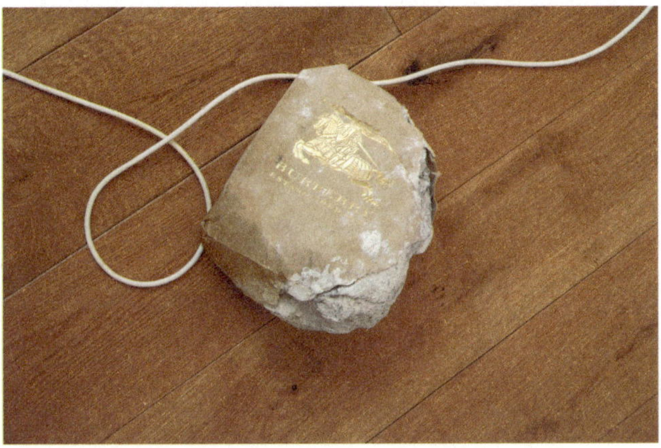

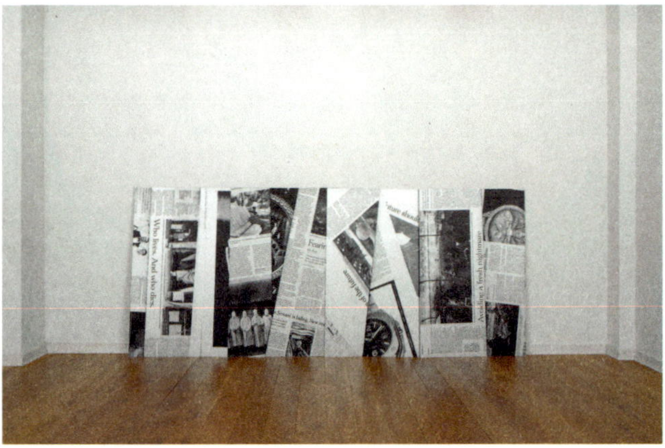

Who lives. And who dies.
of the future
Avoiding a fresh nightmare

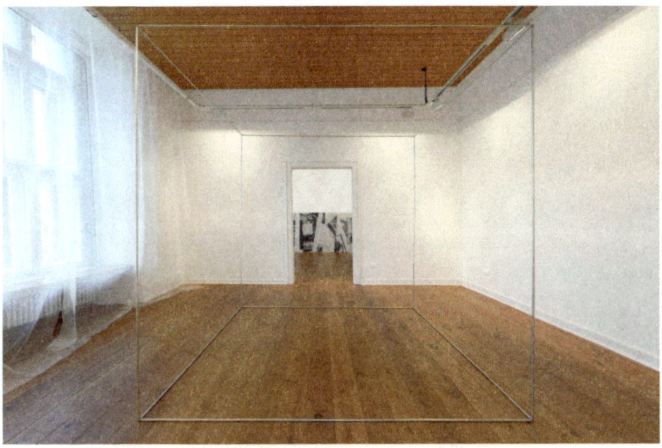

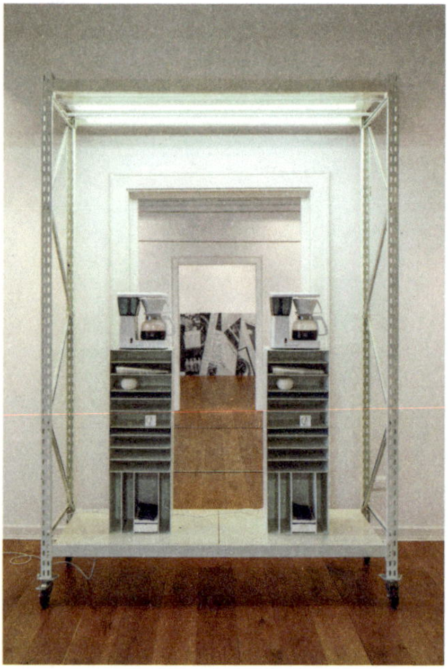

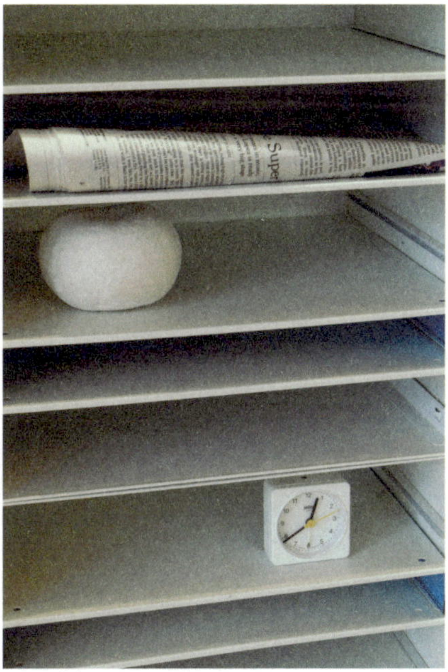

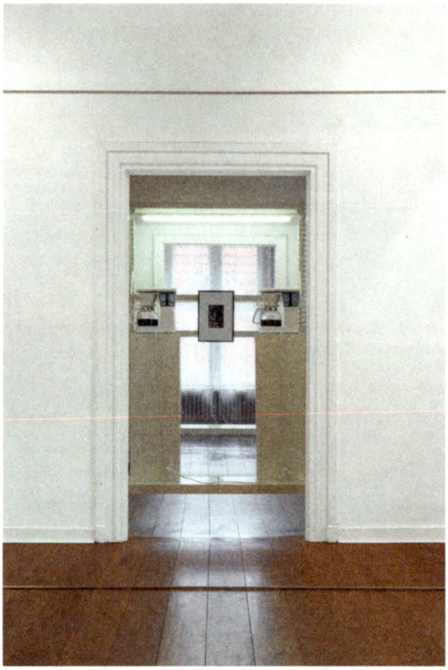

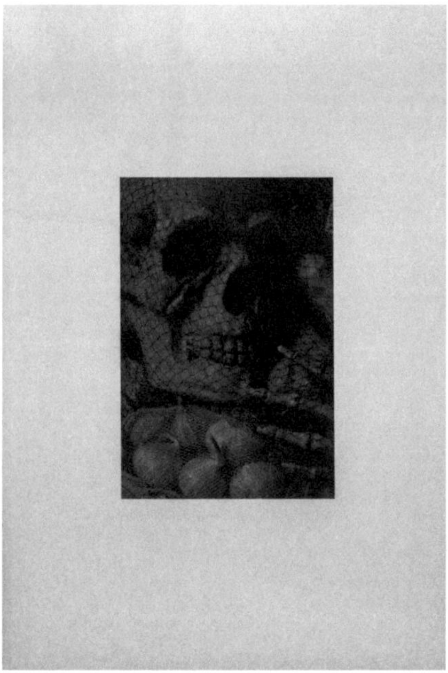

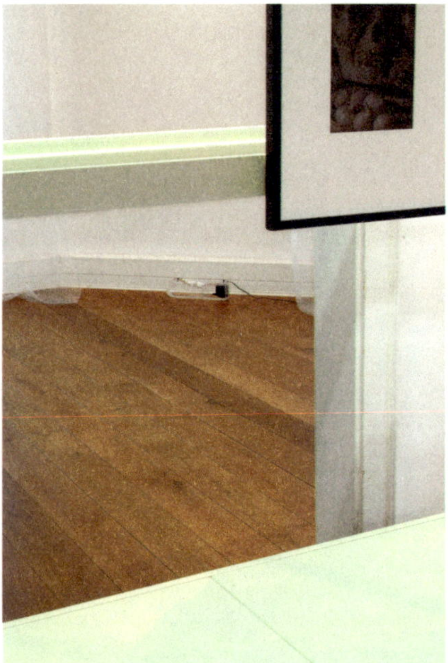

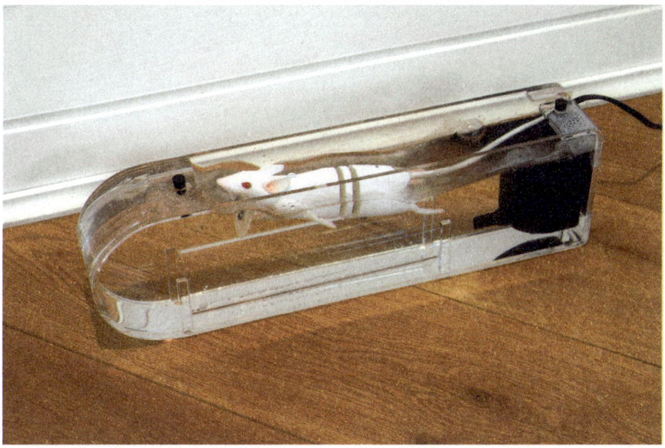

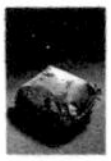

Booster (Audi), 2015
Plaster, aluminium foil, shopping bag
28 x 42 x 9 cm
Rundgang, Städelschule, Frankfurt am Main
Photo: Benedikte Bjerre

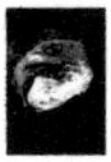

Booster (Hermes), 2016
Plaster, aluminium foil, shopping bag
29 x 31 x 13 cm
Stock'n'flow, Bold Tendencies, London
Photo: Benedikte Bjerre

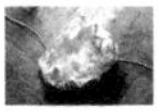

Booster (Burberry), 2016
Plaster, aluminium foil, shopping bag
28 x 25 x 15 cm
Afgang, Charlottenborg Kunsthal, Copenhagen
Photo: David Stjernholm

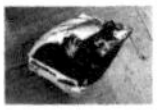

Booster (Plaza), 2016
Plaster, aluminium foil, shopping bag
25 x 35 x 16 cm
Afgang, Charlottenborg Kunsthal, Copenhagen
Photo: David Stjernholm

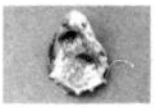

Booster (Nasty Gal), 2016
Plaster, aluminium foil, shopping bag
17 x 35 x 25 cm
31 Women, PPC Philipp Pflug Contemporary, Frankfurt am Main
Photo: PPC Philipp Pflug Contemporary

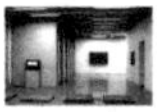

Romancing in thin air, 2015
Aluminium, elastic, Pibella
Ø 1.3 x 3800 cm
PRIMARY STRUCTURES – 1966 bis zur Gegenwart, MMK 2, Frankfurt am Main
Photo: MMK Museum für Moderne Kunst, Frankfurt am Main

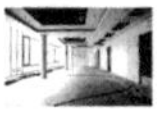

Fat choi spirit, 2019
Aluminium, elastic, flow ink, tennis balls
Ø 1.3 x 3200 cm
Soft City, Coyote, Stockholm
Photo: Ernst Skoog/Coyote

A moment of romance, 2016
Aluminium, elastic
Ø 1.3 x 6400 cm
Stock'n'flow, Bold Tendencies, London
Photo: Benedikte Bjerre

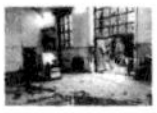

Don't go breaking my heart, 2015
Aluminium, elastic
Ø 1.3 x 3500 cm
Rundgang, The Royal Academy of Arts, Copenhagen
Photo: Benedikte Bjerre

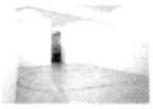

A hero never dies, 2016
Aluminium, elastic, mouthguard
Ø 1.3 x 2500 cm
Trickortreater, Lullin+Ferrari, Zurich
Photo: Lullin+Ferrari

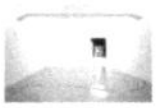

A hero never dies, 2016
Aluminium, elastic, mouthguard
Ø 1.3 x 2500 cm
Trickortreater, Lullin+Ferrari, Zurich
Photo: Lullin+Ferrari

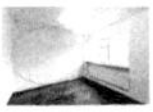

Design for living, 2017
Aluminium, elastic
Ø 1.3 x 2700 cm
Functional-Utility Program, Wschód Gallery, Warsaw
Photo: Wschód Gallery

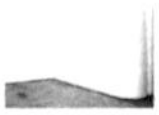

Design for living, 2017
Aluminium, elastic
Ø 1.3 x 2700 cm
Functional-Utility Program, Wschód Gallery, Warsaw
Photo: Wschód Gallery

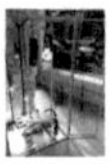

Hotproducts 3, 2016
Powder-coated steel wardrobe, mirror, energy-efficient lightbulbs, hookah hoses, lolliepop displays, wall clock, onion bag, gold coins, booster, brushes, aspirin, spiderman magazin, Rolex
160 x 118 x 80 cm
Trickortreater, Lullin+Ferrari, Zurich
Photo: Benedikte Bjerre

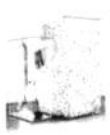

Hotproducts 2, 2016
Powder-coated steel wardrobe, mirror, energy-efficient lightbulbs, hookah hoses, lolliepop displays, transfer print on cotton, Double Cherries
160 x 118 x 80 cm
Afgang, Kunsthallen Charlottenborg, Copenhagen
Photo: David Stjernholm

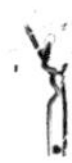

Hotproducts 2, 2016
Powder-coated steel wardrobe, mirror, energy-efficient lightbulbs, hookah hoses, lolliepop displays, transfer print on cotton, Double Cherries
160 x 118 x 80 cm
Afgang, Kunsthallen Charlottenborg, Copenhagen
Photo: David Stjernholm

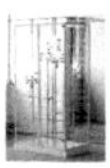

Hotproducts, 2015
Powder-coated steel wardrobe, polystyrene, mirror, tennis ball, lollipop displays, plastelina, strips, cord, light bulb, elastic bungee, plasterboard
101 x 60 x 189 cm
Rundgang, Städelschule, Frankfurt am Main
Photo: Benedikte Bjerre

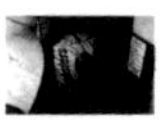

Goods (Live Lobster), 2018
Ink on polyester, chopped foam
60 x 40 x 55 cm
Roots on Wheels, Rootcanal, Amsterdam
Photo: Rootcanal

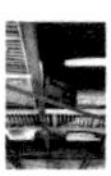

High Hopes, 2018
Ink on polyester, foam, Squishes, IKEA Lönset
146 x 265 x 1046 cm
Perspectives, Kunstfort, Vijhuizen
Photo: Kunstfort

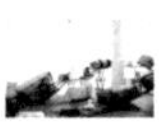

High Hopes, 2018
Ink on polyester, foam, Squishes, Euronorm trays, bronze casts, modified coins, bandage plaster, polystyrene, wood, IKEA Lönset, salon tables
590 x 800 x 789 cm
Good Morning Midnight, De Ateliers Offspring, Amsterdam
Photo: Benedikte Bjerre

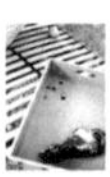

High Hopes, 2018
Ink on polyester, foam, Squishes, Euronorm trays, bronze casts, modified coins, bandage plaster, polystyrene, wood, IKEA Lönset, salon tables
590 x 800 x 789 cm
Good Morning Midnight, De Ateliers Offspring, Amsterdam
Photo: Benedikte Bjerre

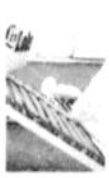

High Hopes, 2018
Ink on polyester, foam, Squishes, Euronorm trays, bronze casts, modified coins, bandage plaster, polystyrene, wood, IKEA Lönset, salon tables
590 x 800 x 789 cm
Good Morning Midnight, De Ateliers Offspring, Amsterdam
Photo: Benedikte Bjerre

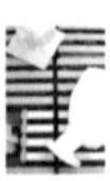

Yomp, 2018
Ink on polyester, foam, Squishes, plaster casts, bandage plaster, styrofoam, IKEA Lönset
150 x 90 x 800 cm
Yomp, Saloon, Brussels
Photo: Saloon/Lola Pertsowsky

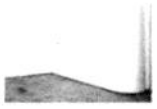

Design for living, 2017
Aluminium, elastic
Ø 1.3 x 2700 cm
Functional-Utility Program, Wschód Gallery, Warsaw
Photo: Wschód Gallery

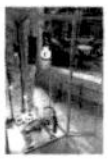

Hotproducts 3, 2016
Powder-coated steel wardrobe, mirror, energy-efficient lightbulbs, hookah hoses, lolliepop displays, wall clock, onion bag, gold coins, booster, brushes, aspirin, spiderman magazin, Rolex
160 x 118 x 80 cm
Trickortreater, Lullin+Ferrari, Zurich
Photo: Benedikte Bjerre

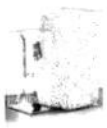

Hotproducts 2, 2016
Powder-coated steel wardrobe, mirror, energy-efficient lightbulbs, hookah hoses, lolliepop displays, transfer print on cotton, Double Cherries
160 x 118 x 80 cm
Afgang, Kunsthallen Charlottenborg, Copenhagen
Photo: David Stjernholm

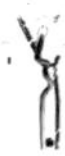

Hotproducts 2, 2016
Powder-coated steel wardrobe, mirror, energy-efficient lightbulbs, hookah hoses, lolliepop displays, transfer print on cotton, Double Cherries
160 x 118 x 80 cm
Afgang, Kunsthallen Charlottenborg, Copenhagen
Photo: David Stjernholm

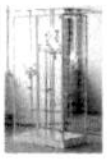

Hotproducts, 2015
Powder-coated steel wardrobe, polystyrene, mirror, tennis ball, lollipop displays, plastelina, strips, cord, light bulb, elastic bungee, plasterboard
101 x 60 x 189 cm
Rundgang, Städelschule, Frankfurt am Main
Photo: Benedikte Bjerre

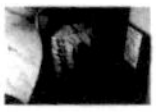

Goods (Live Lobster), 2018
Ink on polyester, chopped foam
60 x 40 x 55 cm
Roots on Wheels, Rootcanal, Amsterdam
Photo: Rootcanal

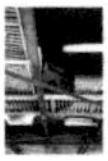

High Hopes, 2018
Ink on polyester, foam, Squishes, IKEA Lönset
146 x 265 x 1046 cm
Perspectives, Kunstfort, Vijhuizen
Photo: Kunstfort

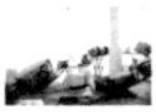

High Hopes, 2018
Ink on polyester, foam, Squishes, Euronorm trays, bronze casts, modified coins, bandage plaster, polystyrene, wood, IKEA Lönset, salon tables
590 x 800 x 789 cm
Good Morning Midnight, De Ateliers Offspring, Amsterdam
Photo: Benedikte Bjerre

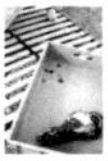

High Hopes, 2018
Ink on polyester, foam, Squishes, Euronorm trays, bronze casts, modified coins, bandage plaster, polystyrene, wood, IKEA Lönset, salon tables
590 x 800 x 789 cm
Good Morning Midnight, De Ateliers Offspring, Amsterdam
Photo: Benedikte Bjerre

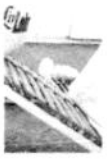

High Hopes, 2018
Ink on polyester, foam, Squishes, Euronorm trays, bronze casts, modified coins, bandage plaster, polystyrene, wood, IKEA Lönset, salon tables
590 x 800 x 789 cm
Good Morning Midnight, De Ateliers Offspring, Amsterdam
Photo: Benedikte Bjerre

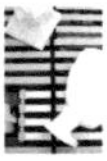

Yomp, 2018
Ink on polyester, foam, Squishes, plaster casts, bandage plaster, styrofoam, IKEA Lönset
150 x 90 x 800 cm
Yomp, Saloon, Brussels
Photo: Saloon/Lola Pertsowsky

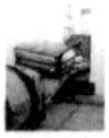

Yomp, 2018
Ink on polyester, foam, Squishes, plaster casts, bandage plaster, styrofoam, IKEA Lönset
150 x 90 x 800 cm
Yomp, Saloon, Brussels
Photo: Saloon/Lola Pertsowsky

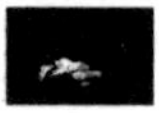

The Comfort of Things, 2017 (with Johannes Büttner and Helge Peters)
Ink on polyester, foam, speaker, Ipod
175 x 45 x 120 cm
The Power Nap, The Stedelijk, Amsterdam
Photo: The Stedelijk

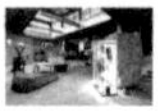

High Hopes, 2018
Ink on polyester, foam, Squishes, Euronorm trays, bronze casts, modified coins, bandage plaster, polystyrene, wood, IKEA Lönset, salon tables
Size variable
Young Danish Art: Forecasting the Future, Arken Museum for Modern art, Ishøj
Photo: Arken Museum for Modern art/David Stjernholm

Goods (Cabin S), 2019/*Goods (Marquet)*, 2017
Ink on polyester, foam
82 x 51 x 37/ 68 x 47 x 37 cm
Architecture Now, La Cucina, Copenhagen
Photo: La Cucina

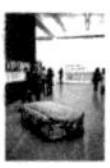

Goods (Trunk), 2018
Ink on polyester, foam
160 x 94 x 84 cm
Klassenverhältnisse – Phantoms of Perceptions, Kunstverein in Hamburg, Hamburg
Photo: John Skoog

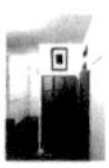

Vanitas-stillevn, 2016
Pigment print on Baryta paper
50 x 35 cm
Private collection, Zurich
Photo: Corrado Ferrari

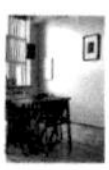

Vanitas-stillevn, 2016
Pigment print on Baryta paper
50 x 35 cm
Last Xmas at the Harbour, private home of Pernille Kapper Williams, Copenhagen
Photo: Pernille Kapper Williams

Rat, 2020
Fly tester, bait, demineralised water
13 x 40 x 8 cm
My dream is longer than the night, Goeben, Berlin
Photo: Stefan Haehnel/Goeben

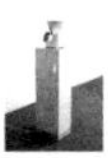

Untitled (Pigeonhole for Karo), 2014
3 IKEA Kvissle lettertray, Melitta Easy, Braun 66031, plaster cast, plexiglas
25 x 32 x 137 cm
Ostersee II, Vesch, Vienna
Photo: Benedikte Bjerre

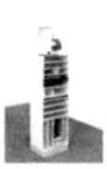

Untitled (Pigeonhole for Karo), 2014
3 IKEA Kvissle lettertray, Melitta Easy, Braun 66031, plaster cast, plexiglas
25 x 32 x 137 cm
Ostersee II, Vesch, Vienna
Photo: Benedikte Bjerre

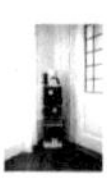

Working Girl, 2015
Powder-coated steel, plexiglass, Falke merino socks, Braun travel alarm, plaster cast, Melitta Easy, filter, water & coffee
25 x 32 x 137cm
Private collection of Friedrich & Johanna Gräfling, Frankfurt am Main
Photo: Lotte Thor

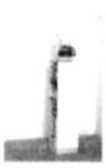

Working Girl, 2015
Powder coated steel, plexiglass, Falke merino socks, Braun travel alarm, plaster cast, Melitta Easy, filter, water & coffee
25 x 32 x 137cm
Rundgang, Städelschule, Frankfurt am Main
Photo: Benedikte Bjerre

His Culture, 2020
Newspaper
17 x 26 cm
die kommende tage, C.C.C., Copenhagen
Photo: C.C.C./ Brian Kure

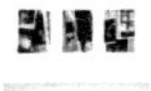

October 22, November 16, December 7 2018, 2019
Laser on natural paper, acid-free tape, collage
113.4 x 80 cm
When facts change I change my mind, Lullin+Ferrari, Zurich
Photo: Lullin+Ferrari

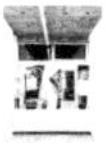

Spring (Days to come), 2020
Laserprint on aluminium
Size variable, here 148 x 245 cm
My dream is longer than the night, Goeben, Berlin
Photo: Stefan Haehnel/Goeben

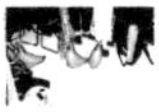

Lisa's chickens (Farm Life), 2016
Foil balloons, cardboard, helium
25 chickens 40 x 40 x 13 cm
Kräftskivan, Galleri Mejan, Stockholm
Photo: Ernst Skoog

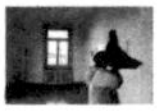

Lisa's chickens (Farm Life), 2016
Foil ballons, cardboard, helium
30 chickens 40 x 40 x 13 cm
Chambers chapter II, Villa Metzlerstraße 21, Frankfurt am Main
Photo: Carina Bukuts/Sonia Knop

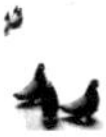

Lisa's chickens (Farm Life), 2016
Foil balloons, cardboard, helium
100 chickens each 40 x 40 x 13 cm
Take me I am yours, Kunsthal Charlottenborg, Copenhagen
Photo: David Stjernholm

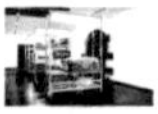

Inventory I-IV, 2021
Powder-coated steel, wheels, LED light, printed polyester, Eurotrays, foam, squishes, modified coins, bronze cast, plaster sculptures, oysterglove, wood, aluminium cast, helium balloons, ladder
4 shelves, each 260 x 170 x 60 cm

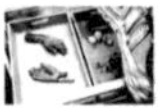

Inventory I-IV, 2021
Powder-coated steel, wheels, LED light, printed polyester, Eurotrays, foam, squishes, modified coins, bronze cast, plaster sculptures, oysterglove, wood, aluminium cast, helium balloons, ladder
4 shelves each 260 x 170 x 60 cm

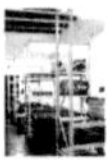

Inventory I-IV, 2021
Powder-coated steel, wheels, LED light, printed polyester, Eurotrays, foam, squishes, modified coins, bronze cast, plaster sculptures, oysterglove, wood, aluminium cast, helium balloons, ladder
4 shelves each 260 x 170 x 60 cm

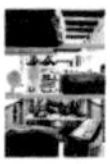

Inventory I-IV, 2021
Powder-coated steel, wheels, LED light, printed polyester, Eurotrays, foam, squishes, modified coins, bronze cast, plaster sculptures, oysterglove, wood, aluminium cast, helium balloons, ladder
4 shelves each 260 x 170 x 60 cm

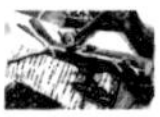

Inventory I-IV, 2021
Powder-coated steel, wheels, LED light, printed polyester, Eurotrays, foam, squishes, modified coins, bronze cast, plaster sculptures, oysterglove, wood, aluminium cast, helium balloons, ladder
4 shelves each 260 x 170 x 60 cm

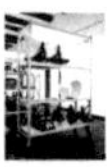

Inventory I-IV, 2021
Powder-coated steel, wheels, LED light, printed polyester, Eurotrays, foam, squishes, modified coins, bronze cast, plaster sculptures, oysterglove, wood, aluminium cast, helium balloons, ladder
4 shelves each 260 x 170 x 60 cm

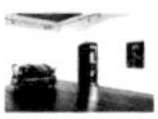

The Rimowas, 2017
Ink on polyester, foam
42 x 105 x 165 / 65 x 105 x 165 cm

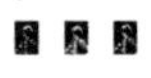

Bettys, 2010
Oil on canvas, in 3 parts
Each 100 x 70 cm

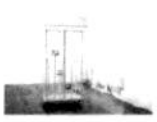

Hotproducts 4, 2021
Powder coated steel, wood, wheels, LED light, mirror, display, lollipop, lock
200 x 180 x 95 cm

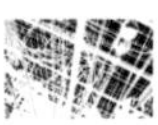

Hotproducts 4, 2021
Powder-coated steel, wood, wheels, LED light, mirror, display, lollipop, lock
200 x 180 x 95 cm

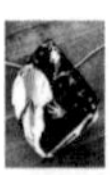

Booster (Plaza), 2016
Plaster, aluminium foil, shopping bag
25 x 35 x 16 cm

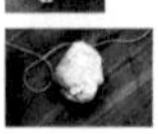

Booster (Burberry), 2016
Plaster, aluminium foil, shopping bag
28 x 25 x 15 cm

Spring (Days to come), 2020
Laserprint on aluminium
Each 148 x 95 cm, together 148 x 350 cm

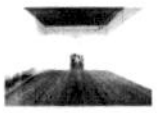

Untitled, 2010/2021
Aluminium, stainless steel
230 x 230 x 230 cm

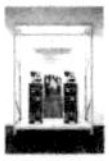

Working Girls in the Age After Reproduction, 2021
Powder coated steel, wheels, LED light, easy coffeemakers, coffee, newspaper, plaster, plexiglass, travel alarm, socks
260 x 170 x 60 cm

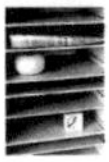

Working girls in the age after reproduction, 2021
Powder coated steel, wheels, LED light, Easy Coffeemakers, coffee, newspaper, plaster, plexiglass, travel alarm, socks
260 x 170 x 60 cm

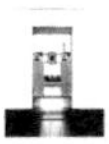

Untitled, 2010/2021
Working girls in the age after reproduction, 2021
JIT, 2021

JIT, 2021
Powder coated steel, wheels, LED light, framed colour photograph
260 x 170 x 60 cm

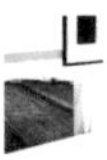

JIT, 2021
Rat, 2020

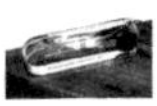

Rat, 2020
Fly tester, bait, demineralised water
13 x 40 x 8 cm

Benedikte Bjerre, *let it go let it go*, Kunstverein Göttingen, Göttingen
Photos: Marius Land, © Kunstverein Göttingen
All works courtesy the artist

Benedikte Bjerre
BB is working with sculpture and installation. Coming to art through sociology and photography, her work engages directly with the movement of objects, capital and humans, in the room, in the network, in the world.

Tomke Braun
Over the last three years TB has been the artistic director of Kunstverein Göttingen. During this period the Kunstverein has presented several new positions of artists who had not yet had an institutional solo exhibition in Germany. BB's exhibition is TB's last at Kunstverein Göttingen.

Rhea Dall
In October 2020 RD finished *Praxes What You Preach*, her PhD at Copenhagen University. It revolved around the exhibition space PRAXES that she co-founded in Berlin in 2013 and the way it engaged directly with an artist practice over a longer period of time rather than for one show only.

Åbäke
Using the components of a book almost as quasi-readymades, Åbäke's work concentrates on the social aspect of graphic design, the power of collaboration and the context specificity of every project.

Benedikte Bjerre
let it go

Editors: Benedikte Bjerre, Tomke Braun
Design: Benedikte Bjerre △ Åbäke
Text contributions: Tomke Braun, Rhea Dall
Proofreading: Tim Schmitt, Daniela Seitz, Susannah Worth
Translations: Milena Maffei, Anna McCarthy
Printing: Grafiche Veneziane

This catalogue is published on the occasion of the exhibition *let it go let it go* by Benedikte Bjerre, Kunstverein Göttingen, Göttingen, 2021.

kunstverein göttingen

Kunstverein Göttingen e.V.
Gotmarstraße 1
37073 Göttingen
Telefon +49 (0) 551 44 899
info@kunstvereingoettingen.de
www.kunstvereingoettingen.de

The exhibition and the catalogue were supported by:

Niedersächsisches Ministerium für Wissenschaft und Kultur

GÖTTINGEN
STADT, DIE WISSEN SCHAFFT

Sparkasse Göttingen
SEIT 1801

Niedersächsische Sparkassenstiftung

Danish Arts Foundation

DANISH ART WORKSHOPS
STATENS VÆRKSTEDER FOR KUNST

The artist would like to thank Kirsten Bjerre, Lullin+Ferrari, John Skoog and Zander Vind.

Published and distributed by
Mousse Publishing – Contrappunto s.r.l.
Corso di Porta Romana 63, 20122, Milan–Italy

Available through:

Mousse Publishing, Milan
moussepublishing.com

DAP | Distributed Art Publishers, New York
artbook.com

Vice Versa Distribution, Berlin
viceversaartbooks.com

Les presses du réel, Dijon
lespressesdureel.com

Antenne Books, London
antennebooks.com

First edition: 2021
Printed in Italy.

ISBN 978-88-6749-465-1
€ 25/$ 29,95